D1603533

How I Conquered
CALL RELUCTANCE,
Fear of SELF-PROMOTION &
INCREASED MY
PROSPECTING!

SIDNEY C. WALKER

Copyright © 2015 by Sidney C. Walker

Published by High Plains Publications
San Diego, California

ISBN: 0-9621177-7-3

Cover Design: Ken Williams, Jr.; GraphicsQuarter.net

Editing: Greg Miller; OtherNetwork.com

Copyediting: Lori Kranz

DEDICATION

Dedicated to those willing to venture outside the confines of the controlling ego to discover the unlimited true Self, who can do anything—*your intuitive spirit.*

TABLE OF CONTENTS

AUTHOR'S NOTES

- The purpose of this book is to create a state of mind for making prospecting calls or taking action on anything you need to do that you are resisting.

- Overcoming fear is a complex subject and there are overlaps or repetition between the different perspectives presented. It is difficult to put all the information into separate compartments.

- Repetition of key concepts from different perspectives increases the likelihood of a breakthrough. Different people need to hear different words for the door to open. I have also found that what worked today may need to be slightly modified for tomorrow. As you change and grow, you need to expand your awareness to diffuse your fear. The key is to find the words, phrases, and concepts that allow you to take action.

- I have purposely not used graphics in order to emphasize what I think is the most important information other than chapter heads, subheads, and occasional italics. I want *you* to decide what's important for *you*. I recommend highlighting as you read to make it easy to find key phrases when you are ready to create your warm-up.

- There is a lot of my personal experience in this book. I am not trying to win you over to my point of view or convince you of anything. My main goal is to help you take action on things you want to do in a way that feels right to you. Don't let an occasional difference in opinion or perspective get in the way of finding what you need to break through. Just take a black marker to the parts you disagree with. I won't mind.

- I have used the term *client* to be synonymous with potential clients, candidates, and all forms of customers.

- I have used the word *advisor* to represent anyone selling any kind of product or service. Everyone is selling or promoting something. In my coaching practice, I teach my clients to be trusted advisors rather than salespeople. I discuss the difference at length.

- I have used the pronoun *they* and its derivatives as much as possible instead of saying *he* or *she*, *him* or *her*. When I do use the pronouns *he* and *she*, I have used *she* intermittently rather than use *he* all the time.

- I have used the word *product* to represent anything you are promoting: product, service, yourself, your ideas, your goals, your agenda, your desires, etc.

INTRODUCTION

It was the spring of 1973. I was about to lose my college deferment from the military draft upon graduation from Michigan State. My lottery number was low and had been called years before. My next address, after a hilltop fraternity house in East Lansing, would be an army barracks in the jungle of Vietnam.

Then on June 19, 1973, the US Congress passed an amendment that would forbid any further US involvement in Southeast Asia. It took a couple of more years to actually end the war. Most important, I graduated from college on June 8 and only had to worry about my future as a soldier for eleven days before I was relieved from military duty.

My thoughts and feelings were going in every direction. Of course, I was elated at the news. I had been preparing for the worst that war had to offer. We had all been made highly aware of the atrocity of war by the army of full-time war protestors in those days. I was an intense twenty-one-year-old with some athletic ability and a short temper. At that time in my life, I would have been a fierce fighter more than a good soldier. I would have likely been overconfident and gotten killed taking risks I didn't need to take just to prove I was fearless.

It was a major blessing that I didn't have to go to war. It felt like a miracle when that ever-present dark reality that had been looming for years, just disappeared. Over 50,000 other souls just like me were not so lucky and another 150,000 were wounded for life. I owe them all for their service and acknowledge that their sacrifice eventually brought the war to an end.

After graduation, I stayed in East Lansing to help a friend build and open an ice arena. Then I spent the winter season managing the ice arena and playing ice hockey with former college stars in the middle of the night. As I pondered my future, everyone said I should be in sales. I think what they meant was I had a knack for promoting things. I had no idea what a sales career would really be like. Life insurance was the only product that held any interest for me and successful agents seemed to have an upscale lifestyle. So I confidently and naively said, "Life insurance it is."

That was the beginning of my lifelong battle with call reluctance and overcoming the fear of self-promotion.

I went to work for my dad's agent in Gross Pointe, Michigan, a wealthy area in north Detroit on the St. Clair River. I rented a room in a mansion close to the office and headed off to the three-day training with four other guys. We learned about insurance products, which were limited compared to today's.

Much of the time was spent learning phone scripts that we endlessly role-played. The prospect's name in all of the scripts was "Bill." I found out later from one of my fellow trainees that when he finally got someone live on the phone for the first time to talk about insurance, he called the guy "Bill" when his name was something else! Hysterical. He didn't get the appointment.

My well-meaning but clueless sales manager, only a couple of years older, had me cold calling rich people about disability insurance starting at 5 p.m. for several hours each night.

That was a nightmare. The first half of my phoning session was having people yelling and swearing at me for calling them during dinner. There were no answering machines back then.

Then the second half was mostly "No, not interested." *Click!* I realized I was not going to be able to do this job, which ruined all my carefully designed plans for the future. I made up excuses why I couldn't make it to the phoning session each night and then proceeded to party and chase women to ease the pain of my first career disaster.

I have done a lot of speaking to financial advisors as a sales coach. When I recounted this story on occasion in front of a group, I would say it took years of therapy to get over that experience. That always got a laugh, as the edge of truth often does. It actually took most of my adult life and a lot of struggle and anguish to conquer my fears and resistance related to making prospecting calls.

Heading back to East Lansing was an obvious move after my cold-calling fiasco in Gross Pointe. I knew hundreds of people from a combination of college and being the commissioner of three men's hockey leagues. I did my best in the life insurance business and got some recognition for several large sales. But after a few years, I knew my call reluctance issue was holding me back and it wasn't going away.

So I tried to branch out. My thinking was that it would be easier to make prospecting calls for other products. I had learned the hard way that discussing your life insurance needs was not the most popular topic of conversation. My new sales manager was also a friend and aware of my dilemma. He had been with Dale Carnegie for many years prior to getting into the life insurance business both as a salesperson and an instructor. He taught me his version of a retail sales training course, which I did for one of my life insurance clients who was involved with a large plumbing and heating company that had retail outlets. They loved what I did and their sales went up noticeably right away.

But even after that great success, when it came time to contact other retail business owners to offer that same training to them…I couldn't pick up the phone.

I had spent weeks learning to do the course, weeks delivering the course, had incredible results, and could not make a single prospecting call to promote it. Then I knew I had a real problem because the product wasn't the issue. My experiences of just a few years had changed me from a hard-charging, ambitious young go-getter into a prospecting chicken.

To make matters worse, I was fervently independent and an innovator at heart. I knew even then I would have difficulty working for someone. I needed to have my own business, which I have managed to maintain for forty-plus years. Of course, I only wanted to promote products that I felt like I had a hand in creating. I was fifteen years ahead of my time as a sales coach and came to discover that promoting a new approach was a much bigger challenge than I had expected.

I had also developed my own approach to the job search process and was doing executive outplacement for Fortune 500 companies before I was thirty.

I stayed involved in the life insurance business as a coach, which eventually grew into speaking and writing books based on my coaching experience with financial advisors. Speaking to large life insurance agencies around the country became a means to attract coaching clients. That combination of activities has kept me employed for decades.

Although I have always struggled with making prospecting calls, I painstakingly got my confidence back over many years from a combination of self-study, coaching others, and getting to the leadership level of a wide variety of awareness trainings, including ten years as a lay monk in a monastery.

Interestingly, I was never able to escape promoting and selling my own products. I have had many periods of success with different but related products along with plenty of those moments when I wanted to quit and do something totally different. But good things always happened when I found a way to attract some new clients and apply my innovative abilities. There was never any other job that felt right to me, even on the worst days.

Then, somewhere along the way, it occurred to me that maybe everything was perfect somehow.

What if one of the things I was here to do was to help people overcome their call reluctance and fear of self-promotion? Maybe I could help them not have to go through what I went through.

I had a similar experience during the earlier years of my coaching career. I had been waiting for my real job to come along. Being a sales coach wasn't considered a career at that point, and even I thought that my avant garde coaching practice would be a stepping-stone to something else. My parents were always wondering when I was going to get a real job. Then, as more and more people found their way to becoming a business coach of some kind, I realized that maybe I had been in the right job all along.

As I look back over my career, I have consistently been drawn to the most challenging aspects of sales and communication. The good news is that I never gave up creating and promoting my own products, and you will be the beneficiary if you keep reading.

What I am about to share with you is timeless and applies to everyone in some way. We are all promoting something and most of us have some form of resistance to doing what we need to do. As the old adage says, "There is nothing new under the sun," but that doesn't mean that people know how to use the information that's available to have a breakthrough. And that is my hope for you, my brothers and sisters: that you have a breakthrough to a new level of peace and prosperity as the result of reading this book.

I am living proof that *anyone* can overcome call reluctance and the fear of self-promotion enough to make the calls you need to make. It is probably more accurate to say that it is difficult if not impossible to get rid of all your fears, doubts, and resistance.

The most important breakthrough comes when you realize that nothing can stop you if you can find a perspective that allows you to take action. And that *bigger perspective* is what I will share with you.

1. WHAT'S POSSIBLE

This book represents over thirty years of research and experience in getting past the barriers that keep you from making the prospecting calls you want to make.

The official title for this sort of thing is *overcoming call reluctance* and *the fear of self-promotion,* which are complex psychological issues. What I have found is that the solutions to getting yourself to risk making more prospecting calls are the same solutions for taking any kind of action where you are experiencing resistance or fear to proceed.

In other words, *this book is a tool to help you increase your ability to do what you need to do in the face of your own resistance.*

What risks do you need to take in life that may be accompanied by resistance? The list is long. Here are a few of the more common examples related to picking up the phone:

• Make a call to promote your product or service…

• Introduce yourself as a potential resource (networking)…

• Make a call to get a job interview…

- Call someone to ask them out on a date…

- Call someone to ask them for a favor…

- Call someone who is upset with you…

- Make a call to deal with a difficult issue you've been putting off…

Most of us have resistance to doing certain things we want or need to do. It is a powerful experience to move past those barriers and take the action you want to take.

To me, the ability to act on what feels intuitively right in spite of any internal resistance is your greatest source of self-fulfillment. It's about being who you really are, rather than settling for less.

Since I have always created and promoted my own products and services, I have had to prospect my whole career, especially for coaching clients. Bottom line: *my personal barriers to prospecting have cost me a lot of money I could have made, and a lot of anxiety.*

The energy you spend not making the prospecting calls you need to make is enormous. You can spend a tremendous amount of time rationalizing and justifying your lack of sales activity. You have to cope with results that are far less than what you are capable of achieving. And the worst part is you spend massive amounts of time dreading making the calls you need to make. I have often said, it takes more energy *not* to prospect than it does to actually make the calls.

Of course, making prospecting calls also *requires* energy. It takes more drive than most other activities, especially in the beginning. It's easy to put off and find other "more important" things to do. I have to gather all my resolve to make the extra effort required to get into action and do what I need to do. It's normal to have to psych yourself up to make prospecting calls and learn to interact with people in an outgoing way if you want to do well.

THE BIG QUESTION

So here's the big question. How bad do you want the things you say you want? Are you willing to do whatever is necessary, within reason, to overcome your barriers to prospecting?

It may seem almost impossible to you now to have a major breakthrough with prospecting, but I assure you it *is* possible if you are willing to learn to think differently and try new things.

The biggest challenge is that we have been trained to think in a way that actually creates call reluctance and fear of self-promotion.

The good news is you can be untrained or unlearn how you relate to prospecting. You can create a mindset that will allow you to set your fears, doubts, and resistance aside and make the calls you need to make or do whatever you need to do.

Getting rid of *all* your fear, doubt, worry, and anxiety—or however you manifest your resistance—is not the goal.

Your best path to success is to diffuse whatever is causing your resistance to the point where it won't stop you. You may always find prospecting a major effort. I still have to push myself to prospect, but I actually now find prospecting to be the simplest part of my job and have found a way to actually enjoy it most of the time.

Prospecting is the most highly paid activity of anything you do in sales and usually the most important activity because it starts the client acquisition process. If you need prospects and you don't do any prospecting, you're going to struggle to stay in business.

For many, prospecting has a big enough payoff that they are willing to put up with some discomfort. The other good news is that even a small amount of regular prospecting goes a long way.

I once heard direct marketing guru Dan Kennedy say there was one little thing he learned to do that made him millions. He said, "Never go home until you have talked to at least one new potential client each day."

That's roughly twenty new people per month. When I first heard Dan say that, I thought, "I can find one person a day." Then I realized that if I added twenty new prospective clients to my inventory each month, I would have the business that I wanted!

The moral of the story is, any increase in your current level of prospecting can have a big impact.

CAN YOU IMAGINE?

Can you imagine what would it feel like to be skilled and confident at prospecting?

Feelings are usually the most motivating thing you can experience. Once I have spent some time interviewing my prospective coaching clients to figure out what they want from a coaching engagement, I repeat back what I have learned from them and ask, "Is this what you want?" They say yes. But it's the next couple of questions that are even more important. Questions like "Are you committed to having the things you say you want, or are they in the 'It would be nice' category?" Most people say they are committed.

Then I ask them how it would feel to accomplish the things they say they want. They respond. Then my final two questions are, "Is that an important feeling for you to have?" and "Are you willing to do whatever is necessary, within reason, to have that feeling?"

How people feel when they have achieved something they really want is a powerful motivator. So let me ask you a few questions that will evoke some feeling.

What are all the things you could have if you didn't have any barriers to prospecting?

Create a list you can review and update, keep adding to it, and keep track of the items you accomplish. I call it a Done List.

It is powerful to occasionally review a list of things you have accomplished. I organize my list by the year. It's human nature to quickly forget about what you've accomplished and focus on what you don't have yet. This is normal, but not an empowering perspective. How would it make you feel to have a whole list of things you have achieved this year that were important to you and yours?

Another tip is to acknowledge all progress. Baby steps lead to success, so the baby steps count.

We will talk more about how to stop negatively judging yourself and your activity or lack of it. That is actually one of the baby steps with the biggest impact. Can you imagine not negatively judging yourself or your sales activity ever again? How would that feel? Do you think that would free up some energy?

If you could find a way to prospect that feels right, how would that feel? If you could find a way to prospect that fits your personal style and strengths and you discovered you could actually do it, how would that feel?

Would you be willing to consider that there are many positive aspects to prospecting that you have not yet had a chance to embrace?

For example, prospecting can be a high. When you are prospecting and having success, there is nothing more fun and invigorating. It's a rush to approach something challenging and experience success.

When you prospect in a way that feels right, it's a great panacea for whatever ails you. You have a better attitude. You have more confidence. You get a spring back in your step.

This doesn't mean that everyone starts saying yes to your offer. But what does happen is that you engage a part of the brain that knows that prospecting is good.

Your controlling, judging, evaluating, analytical ego is usually in a panic. However, your intuitive spirit, who you really are, is much more brave and has access to much greater resources.

One of the most powerful experiences I have ever had was the first time I felt self-sufficient. I knew I could make it in this world, if I could prospect. I knew I could make the money I needed to do the things I wanted, if I could prospect. For me, that was a turning point. That was big.

But I also knew I had some work to do because I had to push myself to prospect. It always felt good to do what I needed to do, but I was surprised at how much energy it took to get on the phone every day. I was determined and scared at the same time. I could see the power of prospecting to achieve my dreams, but I also could see I had barriers in the way. Was there a way for me to overcome my fears and resistance to prospecting so I could have the things I wanted in life?

2. THE REALITY OF PROSPECTING

If you are in direct sales, full-time or part-time; paid by commission, self-employed, or promoting anything, you need to prospect to create new sales. There are exceptions, the main one being that you have enough clients to keep you busy or you have hired someone to prospect for you. For those of us who still need clients and are doing the prospecting ourselves, prospecting is not optional.

Most of us have to motivate ourselves.

Some of you may have a sales manager who makes money when you do. That can be good or not so good, depending on your relationship. Some of you have mouths to feed or at least a significant other to keep happy. So yes, your inner circle is pulling for you and wants you to do well, but for the most part, no one else cares whether you prospect or not. *It's all up to you.*

There can be intense pressure to succeed. You need to make a specific amount of money to make things work. And, if you don't make a certain amount of money, you can lose privileges or even our job. So the pressure is on.

Some people find the need to make money the only motivation they require to be a regular prospector. I call those the lucky ones. But if you are reading this book, the need to make money may not be a big enough motivator to push you to be consistent.

If you have resistance to prospecting, you probably put it off until your back's against the wall and then you get more motivated for a short period. This is totally normal behavior. It makes perfect sense to respond that way. Why would you push yourself to do something you would rather not do?

The problem is that *having* to do something is not usually enough motivation to do what you need to do to get the level of success you desire. In this scenario, prospecting is often something you put up with and can easily put off. So do you think you are ever going to become a regular prospector if it is something you would rather not do? Probably not, and that's a good place to start.

What is your motivation, besides the fact that you need the money?

WHAT MOTIVATES YOU?

You would be surprised at the number of people who don't think they know what really motivates them. I have interviewed thousands of people in my career and regularly ask that question in one form or another. Most people have trouble answering a question beyond the obvious need to make money.

The answer is simpler than you think, and I am going to give you the big-picture answer to speed up the process. You already know this answer to be true, but we lose touch with it.

Our main motivation, underneath all the complexity of life, is that we are here to make the world a better place in some way for those lives we touch. And ideally we want to be of service in a way that best fits our aptitudes, interests, and life goals.

I see people spending hours writing purpose statements with elaborate language and specifics. A purpose statement is a good thing as long as it creates a feeling of motivation. *Feeling* a sense of purpose is more important than having a purpose statement. The purpose statement should be a pointer to the feeling that motivates you.

Author Simon Sinek's strategy is to "Start with Why." I highly recommend his eighteen-minute TED Talk. What he so eloquently points out is that if you know why you are doing something and you tell others that is why you are doing it, they will respond in a much more positive way toward you.

Personally, now I see my service to God and humanity as the rent I pay for my place on Earth. There have been major periods of my life when I was working hard but out of touch with a focus on service, and I was restless, frustrated, and unfulfilled. Of course, not everyone is going to find making the world a better place for others their source of motivation. But for most of us, it's an excellent place to start, especially if you are going to be promoting a product to make other people's lives better in some way.

PROSPECTING REALITIES

To complete our beginning discussion on the basic realities of prospecting, consider the following:

• The activity of prospecting has been around forever. You can prospect for gold, oil, a job, a place to live, a life partner, clients—you name it. Prospecting fits right into our dualistic reality of good and bad, positive and negative, etc. Some people are interested in what we have to offer and some are not. Under the pressure of having to make money, we quickly forget that the possibility for success or failure is what makes life interesting. If everyone we talked to was interested in our product and they all ended up buying, there would not be much challenge involved, which would also mean we would not get paid much for our efforts. One of the reasons direct sales is a highly paid activity is the challenge of prospecting. It's emotionally complex work to find people who are interested in your product mainly because most people are *not* going to be interested, which means you will hear a lot of no's.

- Equally as old as the hills are the established rules that have to be followed to succeed. If you are making up your own rules to override the basic rules of the game, it can be hazardous to your attitude and ultimately to your level of success.

  The most basic rule is that you need to make a certain number of prospecting calls to get certain results. Sure, you can make one call and get lucky, but those odds are not sustainable. If you resist doing the amount of prospecting that you need to reach your goals, you are going to suffer. Not doing enough prospecting is the equivalent of buying lottery tickets to fund your retirement years. The odds are better that you will be struck by lightning. So let's say you can be as creative as you want, but you have to do the activity required to earn a sale.

- To be a good prospector, you have to be a catalyst, a beacon of light that shows people how to have something in their life be more, better, different, easier, cost less, take less time, take less human effort, etc.

- Prospecting is a risk to most people for a variety of reasons we will discuss in detail. Part of the risk is that you are asking people to say yes or no to your offer.

- If you risk doing the required activity of prospecting with moderate skill and the right attitude, you are guaranteed success because a certain number of people are going to buy a useful product or service. Another advantage to consistent prospecting is consistent income. If your prospecting is sporadic, you will see more peaks and valleys in your income.

• The act of calling on prospects is the most significant and profitable activity in sales and promotion. Prospecting starts the process of finding an interested potential buyer. Prospecting shows your commitment to the process—and creates an opportunity. When you make a prospecting call, you are up to bat and now have a chance to get on base or even hit a home run.

You actually make real money with every call, regardless of the outcome. You make more money per second prospecting than any other activity, even if it appears that nothing is happening.

Prospecting is what creates the opportunity for you to earn an income by finding clients who will pay you for your product or service. So if prospecting is what really creates your income, then take the time (number of hours) you prospect and divide it into your income: that is how much you make per hour when you are prospecting. It isn't a perfect analogy, but it's an important perspective to consider.

• Simply stated, the ultimate key to being a successful prospector is not to let anything stop you from making your calls. Unfortunately for many of us, making those calls is much more complicated than "Just do it."

3. THE PROBLEM: YOUR EGO

The main cause of call reluctance and the fear of self-promotion is the ego.

There are different schools of thought on what the ego is and how it works. I will present some basics from my perspective, which is all we need for our purposes here even if some may say it is a bit oversimplified. I'm sure you'll agree your goal is to be able to make prospecting calls, not take a college course on the ego. So here we go.

The ego is born when we are born. The reality we inherit is that we can't take care of ourselves as babies and need the help of adults to survive. The impact of this reality is huge. The main assumption we make is that we need to make sure the adults around us like us in order to survive. So being accepted by other people as a means of survival is one of our first lessons. And it's a powerful lesson that gets reinforced by society in a variety of ways throughout our lives.

To a great extent, our ego is formed by how others feel about us. This is shocking if you think about it. A primary part of who we think we are, the basis for how we live our lives, is based on a collection of other people's opinions, not our own. When we are born, we are not aware of ourselves—that comes later. Our first awareness is of everyone and everything other than ourselves. We eventually start to identify ourselves by contrast to all that is outside of us or *not us*.

As the child has more and more contact with people, a functional version of who we think we are is formed, but it is only a reflection of what others think about us; it is not who we really are. This is why the ego is called the *false self,* or *pseudo self.* Who we really are has to come from *within,* which is not based at all on other people's opinions. So now the players have been announced. You have the ego, which is based on a collection of other people's thoughts about you, and your true self or what I like to call your *intuitive spirit,* which is based on an inner you that was not created as a reaction to other people's opinions.

The ego also has other jobs that are related to our discussion. The ego's job is to protect us from potential harm— basically—to keep us alive. The ego works with memories of potentially dangerous experiences. If the ego sees or perceives something happening or about to happen that reminds it of a past dangerous situation, it does what it can to stop us from taking any kind of action other than to withdraw. To fight back is another option the ego might consider in order to protect us, but let's leave that option off the table for now since it doesn't really apply to this discussion.

So by getting us to move away from the danger, the ego is doing it's job to assure our survival in a world full of traps and snares.

The ego is extremely intelligent and crafty. It is as smart as you are on your best day. And your ego will use any means it can dream up to keep you from taking action that it would consider dangerous in some way. After all, to your ego your survival is a life or death matter that it does not approach lightly.

YOU ARE THE CHOOSER

Your level of awareness and personal development will determine how much your relate to yourself as your ego.

Many people don't see much more than their ego sees. Your ego is a highly integrated part of you that can feel so familiar you may think that it is who you are. But the reality is you have the capacity to be much more if you learn to identify the ego's limited agenda and replace it with a more intelligent version of yourself.

The best evidence that you are not your ego is that you can choose to go against the ego's advice. If you can recognize that your ego is telling you to stop doing something that is potentially dangerous, like making prospecting calls, you don't have to stop if you don't want to. So who is it that is saying no to the ego's warning? Who is making a decision to do something different than what the ego wants you to do? It's like the old cartoons that show the devil on one shoulder whispering into one ear and an angel on the other shoulder whispering into the other ear. Most of the time, the selfish, controlling, and cunning ego is going to sound more like the devil than like the angel.

The ego relates to the physical body as who we are. The ego's concept of reality is that we have a body and we are separate from everyone else because that is how it appears in physical reality. Everyone has their own body. However, we are not limited to the ego's reality of being a separate physical body. We have other realities, like that of being a spirit that is connected to other people and other things in some way. We will discuss the reality of spirit more later.

The most important thing to see at this point is that we have a reality that is created by the part of us we call the ego and we can go against its advice if we want. The reason this is important is that if you can argue with your ego or go against its advice, you are not your ego. You are something bigger. I like to say, who we really are is the *chooser*.

You can choose the thoughts and feelings you want to have at any time, any place, regardless of the demands of the voices in your head. Certainly there are many powerful, programmed responses that you have to contend with and it can look like you don't have any choice. But who you really are has the potential to choose to think and feel whatever you want, as outrageous as that may sound.

People who are not familiar with the idea that you are the chooser will argue that what you think and feel just happens and you don't really have any choice about it. That is how it appears at first glance. It is a big step in awareness to realize that you have more control than you may have ever realized, and this is extremely useful in our mission to overcome call reluctance and the fear of self-promotion.

EXTENSIVE MEMORIES

We carry around endless memories of our own experience in the database of our mind. Some say that we also carry around the memories from past lives, if you believe in that sort of thing. A more scientific explanation of past lives is that we inherit the memories of our parents at the time of conception. Our parents also inherited the memories of their parents. That would mean that each one of us could have the memories of the thousands of people in our family tree dating back as far as you can imagine, passed on at the time of their conception. We may not get all the memories of each couple, but we get all the memories up until the time their child is conceived.

These memories are not in our conscious mind. We wouldn't know what to do with all that information. But some would say that all that information is in our subconscious mind.

The important thing to consider is that when you are afraid of something that is happening or could happen, you are not reacting to just one incident in present time. The way the ego works to protect us, it is more likely reacting to the memory of many similar past dangerous experiences, not just the one we are currently facing. If you are reacting to many related fearful situations, your reaction is going to be much more intense.

Functionally, you have to find the courage in the face of danger in order to take action. I bring up these ideas here as potential explanations for the intensity of our fears or resistance.

When we make a prospecting call, what is the real danger? Physically there is no risk. Then why do we have so much fear about making the call? Why can the fear of dialing the phone have the intensity of a life or death situation? To our ego it may actually look like a life or death situation. So it is going to respond accordingly with everything it's got to keep us safe. Don't worry; there are ways to diffuse the fear whether you are dealing with one incident in your mind or many.

Fortunately the system works in reverse. If you can release yourself from the fear of the moment, you can release yourself from all the seemingly related fears as well. These are intriguing possible answers for why some of our fears are so intense in the face of what may be in this reality a minor, momentary discomfort or no real danger at all.

JUDGE AND EVALUATE: THE EGO'S JOB

Let's look more at how the ego protects us from present danger or perceived potential danger.

The main weapon in the ego's arsenal is judgment and evaluation. That is how the ego was created, by other people's judgment and evaluation. Did you ever notice that there is a voice in your head that is constantly judging and evaluating everything that is going on around you? Your ego would rather that you not know what its voice sounds like. If you learn to challenge or ignore the constant protective chattering of your ego, it becomes a much bigger challenge for your ego to control you in its mission to keep you safe.

Here's how it works. You get ready to make some prospecting calls or decide it's time to make a challenging call that you've been putting off. Your ego accesses all your memories in a split second. It reminds you of all the things that have gone wrong in the past or could go wrong now.

Sometimes you may only feel intense anxiety and not anything specific. As I mentioned, the ego is amazingly creative and cunning. It will throw everything at you it can dream up to keep you from taking action if it thinks the action you want to take is potentially dangerous to your survival or comfort level.

Below are some examples of what the ego might be saying to you as you get ready to dial. I started many of the phrases with "I." Your ego wants you to think that what it's telling you is the real you and these thoughts are totally logical reasons not to make the call(s).

• "I'm not ready to make these calls."

• "I'm not sure what to say to this person."

• "I don't have the right language to make these calls."

• "I can make these calls tomorrow. There are other more important and more immediate things to do."

• "This probably isn't the best time to make these calls."

• "This person probably doesn't need what I am offering."

• "This list of prospects isn't any good."

• "I need to come up with a better offer."

• "I would call these referrals, but then I would be out of referrals."

• "There has to be an easier way."

- "I think I will find a way to prospect besides using the phone."

- "Maybe I can find a good book on how to overcome call reluctance."

- "I'm feeling hungry. I think I'll have an early lunch."

The potential list of thoughts the ego will produce to either distract you or somehow keep you from dialing the phone (or anything that appears to be potentially dangerous) is endless.

We know that the ego is afraid that something bad might happen based on its collection of past experiences and it wants to protect us. Here is a partial list of the fears the ego is responding to:

- Fear of rejection or being negatively judged by others in some way

- Fear of failure or incompetence or being taken advantage of

- Fear of embarrassment or of being laughed at

- Fear of feeling stupid or inadequate

- Fear of being wrong or blindsided

- Fear of looking bad or looking like an idiot

- Fear of the unknown or of the unforeseen

- Fear of change, or of something new, or of success

If you attempted to include every possible thing you could be afraid of, the list is going to be a long one and different for each person. The good news is that dealing effectively with a few of the bigger fears takes care of the little ones.

FEAR AND PRESSURE

How are we taught to deal with fear and pressure? Our academic training from first grade to adult education teaches us to solve problems with analysis and linear logic. This approach is based on what is *observably true and provable* based on what appears to be the facts.

Life is much more complicated than this model because there are many powerful elements that cannot be seen. Consequently, the academic model doesn't work well with anything complicated or fast moving. The academic approach is good for adding a column of numbers where there is a narrow focus, no moving parts, and no rush. But when you add people to the equation, which adds a high level of complexity, the analytical approach is painfully slow, plodding, and prone to mistakes due to its limited perspective.

If the problem is more complicated than the analytical model can handle, you won't come up with an answer that will work and surely not in a short amount of time.

Albert Einstein said, "You can't solve the problem with the same paradigm that created the problem." You have to shift to a bigger perspective or bigger paradigm so you can see more. If you are lost, it can help to get to higher ground so you can see more of your surroundings. If you have a big enough perspective, you can effectively deal with a more complicated problem. Einstein knew how to shift to a bigger perspective and subsequently came up with solutions to some of the most complex questions of our physical world.

The most important thing to consider is that we are much more likely to be able to solve any problem if we shift to a bigger perspective.

Here are some examples of analytical solutions that sound good but don't help much.

• Just make more calls and your fear will go away.

- You can't care about what people think of you.

- You have to really believe in what you are selling (promoting).

- That person has your money in his wallet and your job is to get it.

- If what you are selling is worthwhile, everyone should want it!

There is some truth to these statements, but because the analytical focus is so narrow, these well-meant suggestions don't do much to inspire you to prospect if you are feeling some resistance. You need more horsepower; you need a much bigger perspective.

A fascinating thing happens when you combine the analytical approach with the ego. It creates a righteousness about the information the ego has collected about how life works.

Remember, the ego is naturally overly dramatic—everything is a life or death issue. It's all about survival, avoiding risk, avoiding discomfort, and staying safe. Further manifestations of the ego and its desire to be right about its information bring in a desire to control everything or even dominate. The ego will do everything it can to make sure it gets its way. If pushed, the ego doesn't care about anyone else, only its survival, which also means it has to be right. If you argue with the ego about how it thinks life works based on the information it has collected (true or false), you are in for a major battle with a highly skilled opponent.

Furthermore, your analytical ego is obsessed with doing everything perfectly or exactly the way it should be done to fit the information it has collected. It then constantly judges and evaluates how you're doing in relation to it's library of past experiences.

The analytical ego assumes that if you are doing it correctly, everyone will say yes or everyone will buy. If what you do or the action you take doesn't work somehow, you must have done something wrong. So now your own ego, which is trying to protect you but has a limited view of reality, is making *you* the reason its brilliant information didn't work. You did it wrong! This, of course, makes you go back to the drawing board to figure out what went wrong. Victory again for the ego. *Remember, to the ego, it has succeeded if it can keep you off the phone trying to figure out what went wrong.*

So now you are getting ready to make a prospecting call. You are scared about what could happen based on memories of past negative experiences. You are now also afraid that you may do it wrong and really screw things up. Your dedicated ego is going to do everything it can to keep you off the phone in order to avoid the perceived danger, and it is willing to fight ferociously to do it. Most people have no idea what they are up against when they decide to take a sales job or try to promote something, anything.

The ego's obsession with constantly judging and evaluating how we are doing against its notes on how things are supposed to work creates another titanic problem. We negatively judge the process of prospecting, which makes us want to stop and try to fix what's wrong.

YOUR EGO'S APTITUDE

Another formidable aptitude of the ego is its ability to make things up that sound true based on a tiny bit of information. Your ego can enlist the help of your analytical mind and your imagination, then look at a person's address and, based on the neighborhood they live in, make all kinds of logical assumptions. You will have thoughts floating into mind like "Since they live in a nice neighborhood, they must have money. Since they have money, they must be smart. Since they are smart, they probably already have a financial advisor [or fill in the blank with any product or service]. I guess there's no reason to call them."

Does the ego actually know for a fact that any of this information is true about this person? No. Is it possible that the ego's assumptions are totally wrong? Yes.

One thing you will learn if you haven't already is that when you phone a prospect, you have no idea how the call is going to go, regardless of what your ego has told you. If you have never met the person you are calling, your ego has no clue about what the conversation will be, but it will make you think it does in order to keep you from making the call!

Remember, if your ego has decided that making prospecting calls is potentially dangerous, it has to find a reason not to make the call. Then it has done its job to protect you. Obviously, not making any prospecting calls is going to cause you to be short on money, so is that really protection in the long run? Unfortunately, the ego doesn't think that far into the future. The most important thing to the ego is to get rid of the immediate threat. It will worry about the bigger problems later.

I was traveling along the East Coast one summer with some friends when I was in college. We were momentarily excited to come across a bar that had a big sign out in front that said: *FREE BEER TOMORROW*. Our analytical egos were momentarily looking forward to the free beer tomorrow.

Then we shifted to a bigger perspective and realized there would be no free beer because in this case, tomorrow never comes. The ego likes to push off the bigger problems until tomorrow so it can deal with the immediate problems of right now. In this way, the ego never gets around to dealing with the real problems until it's too late.

The ego has plenty of positive qualities. It keeps us alive and breathing. It protects us and fights for us in many ways. The ego makes us fight to survive. It fights for what we believe in to a certain extent. Of course, your ego is going to be more excited about fighting for what *it* believes in based on its programming and experiences. If you decide to pursue a path that could be dangerous, your ego is going to let you know it is having second thoughts, and that can be a good thing.

But here is the big problem presented by the ego. It is the source of most of our suffering. If we are not aware of how the ego can get in our way, we can end up letting a tiny, myopic, overprotective, scared part of our psyche keep us from getting what we want in life. When it comes to overcoming call reluctance and the fear of self-promotion, the ego is in way over its head and has no idea how to deal with the problem other than to do what it has always done: make the threat go away by not prospecting!

The ego actually *is* the problem and you can't get rid of your ego. It is a permanent part of who you are. The problem can be solved, but I hope you are starting to see it's going to take some skill to outsmart the wily ego.

– THE NEGATIVE SPIRAL –

You are dialing the phone and noticing that your ego is negatively judging the prospecting process, which makes you doubt what you are doing and how you are doing it. For example, if you make a call and someone says, "No, they are not interested." To the analytical ego, this is not possible. We must be doing something wrong. We have a product that everyone should want. How is it possible that someone could say no? If you get three no's, in a row, the analytical ego will start to make you think that maybe this isn't as good of a deal as you may have thought.

When you negatively judge something, it creates a negative vision of what is happening or of what could happen. Once you have created a negative vision, the ego has reason to doubt or fear and the alarms go off. Protection is needed to make sure that the organism survives. That protection usually manifests itself in the form of avoiding any further action (no more prospecting) until you can eliminate the risk or take the potential for discomfort away.

24

Once you have allowed a negative vision to creep into your awareness, all kinds of other negative visions can enter. You will question whether you have the right phone approach. You start to consider that people are not actually interested in the product or service you are offering and that maybe you need to represent a different product. It doesn't take long before the doubt you are feeling about what you are doing for a living will stop you from prospecting altogether. You may consider that you need to change jobs and do something different.

Your analytical ego wants to either fix what is wrong with what you are currently doing or find another way to prospect. Either way, the net result is that you stop prospecting, which solves the short-term problem for the ego: to get rid of the fear, the risk, the discomfort, the worry, the anxiety. Then the ego has done its job to protect you from the immediate danger.

The bigger problem is that you are left with major doubt about everything related to prospecting. If there is doubt or fear, your resistance to prospecting is going to be strong and you will find something else to do.

In my several decades as a sales performance coach, I have seen this negative judging of the prospecting process stop successful salespeople dead in their tracks. It can start with a major negative event in their life: a failure of some kind, financial pressure, a divorce, sickness, injury—anything that can take a person's confidence away and make them hesitant or afraid to take risks.

When people are faced with highly negative situations, they project possible negative outcomes into the future and then become extremely cautious. Since prospecting requires an element of risk, the willingness to prospect either slows way down or stops altogether. Once the prospecting stops, so does new income, which usually means the problems and complications continue to escalate.

I have seen many people wait until their back is against the wall and then have an intense flurry of prospecting activity until they get enough money coming in to take the pressure off. Then they go back to putting off prospecting for as long as possible. I did that myself for many years. It's no fun. It's a debilitating and demeaning feeling not to have the income you are capable of earning.

If you are negatively judging making calls or any part of the prospecting process, you will never make enough calls to make it work without some major luck. Even if you are lucky once in a while, you will eventually find that not making enough calls means you are going to struggle to make enough sales.

4. SALES PHILOSOPHY

I'm not big on trying to push people to do things. When I was being trained to sell life insurance, they would say things like "Get at least five no's on the phone before you give up." That reminded me of an old country-western song title, *What Part Of No Don't You Understand?*

You can tell when someone is not interested and when there is some room to keep going with the conversation. This brings us to the topic of differences in selling style, which are important to address because they can greatly affect your ability to make prospecting calls.

TWO BASIC SELLING STYLES

What follows is an oversimplification, but you will get the idea. There are two basic kinds of salespeople: *Client Controllers* and *Relationship Builders*.

Very simply, Client Controllers are going to do everything imaginable to make the sale. They think their job is to make the sale no matter what. In their world, if they don't make the sale, they have failed. So the Client Controller is determined to talk the client into a corner they cannot escape from and get the check.

On the other side is the Relationship Builder, which is a very different species. The Relationship Builder is a lover not a fighter. My Relationship Builder coaching clients would say that they care more about the client than about making a sale. In other words, how the prospective client feels about them is more important than whether they buy anything. The hope is that if you develop a good relationship with the prospective client, they will consider you as their resource and buy from you when the timing is right.

I am a champion of the Relationship Builder or low-key approach. It is a theme you will sense throughout this book. SellingWithoutWrestling.com is an extensive website I've developed for financial advisors. Some of the language is in the context of financial services, but much of it is generic. It is relatively easy to modify my language to work for your product or service. There is a 7-day Free Trial so you can check it out for free to see if it is a resource that would be helpful to you.

One of the most important observations from my thirty years as a coach to financial advisors is this: *The average closing ratio of a skilled Client Controller is 30 percent. The average closing ratio of a skilled Relationship Builder is 90 percent.*

Client Controllers tend to do well because they are often fearless prospectors. They live to conquer people. But they have to prospect three times harder than the Relationship Builders for the same money. Another way to say it is that Client Controllers tend to be bridge-burners while Relationship Builders are bridge-builders. If you don't buy from a Client Controller the first time around, you are in the enemy camp of people who didn't buy. I don't consider that way of thinking wrong as much as not an approach I would be comfortable using knowing what I know.

Another observation from my research worth mentioning is that when you take a Relationship Builder approach, you have a lot more repeat sales and a lot more unsolicited referrals. Most Client Controllers don't care much about repeat sales.

They are usually going for the biggest onetime sale they can make or even a one-call close. Also, Client Controllers typically don't get unsolicited referrals. A Client Controller is not usually someone you would introduce to your friends and family without some pressure from him. Even then, you would think twice before unleashing the Client Controller on the people you care about. The most important thing is that you get to decide which approach best fits your values. Both approaches create sales.

SELLING STYLE CAN AFFECT CALL RELUCTANCE

The selling style you adopt can greatly affect your call reluctance and your fear of self-promotion. Most of us have been taught to be Client Controllers. Most of us don't actually like the idea of having to control people to make a sale, but we are taught that is what we have to do to succeed. We assume this is the approach other people are taking so we do our best to learn the Client Controller approach.

The Client Controller approach has clearly defined steps:

1. Get an appointment however you can. It doesn't matter if the prospect is not that interested because the strategy is to make every attempt to get them interested in your product when you meet. You try to establish a need in the mind of the prospect for your product. You tell them all about your product and all its wonderful benefits.

2. Start the closing process, which is a variety of techniques to get the prospect to make a buying decision. If your prospect has objections to buying your product, you are taught how to deal with these objections and see if you can answer the objections well enough for the prospect to consider buying your product.

3. Finally, use any number of closing techniques designed to get the prospect to start filling out the paperwork. As you know, this approach can be a major back and forth battle. It

can easily turn into a wrestling match designed to ware the prospect down to the point where they will write the check.

With the Client Controller approach, making the sale is more important than the wants and needs of the prospect. If the client objects and gives you a reason why he or she doesn't want to buy, your job is to overcome that objection. So making the sale is everything. If you don't make the sale, you have failed. A similar attitude exists with telephone prospecting as a Client Controller. If you don't make the appointment when you initially talk to someone, you have failed.

Now let's summarize the steps of the Relationship Builder approach so you can see the difference.

1. The first big difference is related to prospecting. With the Relationship Builder approach, your goal is not just to make an appointment. The prospect has to have expressed some interested in your offer or you don't want to proceed. The reason there has to be some interest in your offer is that as a Relationship Builder, you are not going to take a prospect who is not interested and try to turn them around. That is too controlling and too adversarial. When you prospect as a Relationship Builder you are usually offering an educational process that will help the prospect make a more informed decision about the product you are offering.

2. Next you spend time getting to know your prospect by asking a lot of questions about them and their situation. In the process of taking a sincere interest in the prospect by your interviewing skills, a rapport and a level of trust begin to form. How you set up the relationship in the beginning is key. You make it clear to the prospect early in the conversation that they don't have to buy anything for you to be friends and for you to help them. The level of trust skyrockets when you take this approach.

3. You continue your interviewing and educational process to discuss the future issues your prospect is going to face that

could be affected by your product. You find out what they care about and what they don't care about. You get the things they don't care about off the table and then develop strategies to address the issues they do care about. You educate them on the options they have to address their specific issues and build the best solution together as a team.

4. Finally, you help the prospect make an informed decision about whether they should proceed to buy your product or not based on whether they feel it is a good match for their situation. If it doesn't feel right for any reason, you see if you can resolve the issue and get it to feel right. If you can't resolve the issue, you are done and you part friends. You have succeeded in helping the prospect make an informed decision about whether your product is a good match for them.

The big difference with the Relationship Builder approach is that you have succeeded without having to make a sale.

You succeeded at helping your prospect make an informed decision that feels right to them. You have a new relationship with someone who has a level of trust of you and your approach. You have a prospect who may buy from you in the future and may be willing to refer you to others right then.

With the Relationship Builder approach, the prospect is empowered at the end of the process if they didn't buy. If the prospect does battle with a Client Controller and doesn't buy, the prospect is more likely to be glad the meeting is over and hope not to have to deal with that person again.

So here is the key question: With your values, are you going to be more comfortable prospecting as a Client Controller or a Relationship Builder? Both approaches create sales but they are very different. You have to decide what feels right to you at the deepest level.

For me, the choice is clear. I have been both a Client Controller and a Relationship Builder. I could never go back to being a Client Controller with what I know now. I like having an extremely high closing ratio without being pushy or controlling. I like having clients who enjoy having me be part of their lives and who refer me to their friends and family. I like the feeling I get helping people make informed choices that feel right to them. I like who I get to be as a Relationship Builder a lot more than being a Client Controller.

The most important thing here is that you get to choose who you want to be and how you want to approach prospecting and selling.

WHAT IF

Here is a piece I wrote to get people thinking about the power and simplicity of the Relationship Builder approach. It is a different approach. It takes some getting used to. You have to try it.

It takes guts to let go of trying to control the client and switch to helping them make an informed decision that feels right to them. If you have made money with a particular approach, even if it hasn't worked very well, it can be a challenge to give it up for something that works far better. You have to trust your intuitive instincts. Your ego doesn't want to make any changes!

– What If –

What if the best way to make sales is not what we've been trained to think?

What if the conventional wisdom about what makes people buy is actually what is holding us back from our real potential? (At one point the conventional wisdom was that the world was flat!)

What if we have been misled to think that the only way to make sales is to talk people into buying things?

What if the reality is that people want to buy products and just need legitimate help in discovering what they want to buy?

What if our discomfort with prospecting is the result of a misunderstanding of how the sales process really works?

What if our job is simply to offer our ability to help people and see who wants our help?

What if all you need to do is to present the opportunity of working with you and the right people will say, "Yes, I would like some help."

What if you can't say the wrong thing to the right person?

What if your clients are waiting for you to call on them and present the opportunity to work together?

What if the thing people really want from you is to show them how your product might help their situation without any pressure to buy?

What if your job is to simply help people make informed decisions that feel right to them?

What if the best way to double your income is to simply help people make an informed decision about whether to buy your product or not without any sales pressure?

What if most of the sales process is really out of your control and you have been taught to try to control it?

What if trying to control what people do actually makes people find more reasons *not to buy* than reasons *to buy*?

What if the main reason people don't buy is that they feel you are trying to sell them what *you* want them to have rather than what *they* want to buy?

What if sales pressure makes your prospects feel like you care more about the commission than about helping them get what they want?

What if the number of people who will buy doubles when you take away the sales pressure?

What if the approach you were taught is really not the most effective?

What if you made the most important part of your job to help people make informed decisions that feel right to them? Is there any way that could fail?

What if the Universe stands by watching to see how you approach people and rewards you according to your approach?

What if you actually could not fail if you let go of trying to control the process?

What if your ability to go to the next level in your practice is the willingness to let go of trying to control the process and simply help people make educated decisions that feel right to them, which includes doing nothing?

What if prospecting and making sales is really much easier than you ever imagined and you've been taught to make it hard and complicated by well-meaning but misguided people who are unknowingly attached to an approach based on scarcity?

What if all you need to do to make more sales is trust your instincts, trust your heart, teach people what they need to know to make a good decision, and then help them get what feels right to them?

What if you are missing out on great wealth, the smiling faces of happy clients, and your own peace of mind due to a small misperception?

What if all you ever wanted from your career, is just a new thought away?

What if I'm right? Are you willing to let go of your fears, your doubts, your skepticism, your proof that it can't be that easy, and risk giving it a try?

What if all you need to do is to trust and act on what feels deeply right to you and stop listening to what others think?

Your ego is likely telling you this approach is nonsense; your intuitive spirit is likely telling you there is truth here! You are the chooser and you are the only one in the world who knows what feels intuitively right for you.

5. SOLUTIONS FROM A BIGGER PERSPECTIVE

The purpose of this chapter is to present concepts that will help you learn to maintain a bigger perspective that will reduce your fear and consequent resistance to making prospecting calls.

I have described nine of the most fruitful concepts I have found for making you an unstoppable prospector. Let's start with the VAA Formula, which is an extremely effective model for creating anything you want.

THE VAA FORMULA

In the mid 1980s I met an important mentor by the name of Kurt Wright who was a leading management consultant to Fortune 100 executives. We became friends and I ended up traveling with him to do his *Clear Purpose Management* program for the top 10 percent of the executives of major companies.

I learned many useful things from Kurt, plus we had a lot of fun together coaching top executives. One of my favorite coaching sessions was with a company president in his private dining room with massive picture windows and awe-inspiring views. The three of us sat down for lunch. The waiter gave us that day's menu with several choices. I felt like royalty. We were overlooking a vast lagoon linked to the ocean. Several times during lunch, dolphins swam by and jumped out of the water to show off. We had a successful coaching session in which I played a key role. That was one of my top five most spectacular lunches.

The most important thing I learned from Kurt is what I now call the VAA Formula. This is my own version of what Kurt taught me, as I have expanded on the formula over the years.

First you have to *get your formula down to three parts*. He used to say, "People think in threes and the formula will work best if they only have to remember three things." I spent many years learning, coaching, and doing research on overcoming psychological barriers of all kinds. When Kurt said your formula has to be in three parts, I found a way to put all the important information I had gathered under three headings and have successfully used this formula in my coaching practice since that time.

There are a variety of words you could use for the three headings of the formula. The words I have been the most comfortable with are *Vision, Action, Attitude* (VAA), hence the VAA Formula.

This is a formula for creating anything you want to create in this reality. It is profound and bulletproof. It always works, but that doesn't mean there won't be challenges along the way and lots of trial and correction.

– *VISION* –

Vision is the first part. A vision can be a target, a goal, a purpose, a mission, a possibility, or any kind of desired outcome. A vision can be something you want to happen in the next five minutes or the next five years. It can be like a canvas with a few colors and outlines on it while the rest is blank. Or it can be like an architectural drawing with every aspect figured out in exact detail. A vision gives you a destination to move toward, like a North Star to follow in the sky.

A vision is typically something that you can see, but for those who are not as visual, it can be a feeling or a set of words, or even a sound or any combination of the five senses. The concept of a vision is dynamic and limited only by the imagination of its creator.

One time Kurt said to me, "I have decided to become Governor of Colorado." We were both living in Denver at the time. I responded with a look of disbelief and said, "Really?" He thought for a few seconds and then responded, "Well, probably not. But I like the way it makes me feel. It's a good vision for me."

Once you have a vision, the idea is to *hold* the vision of what you want to create in your mind's eye or in your heart, or both, until it becomes a reality. We don't know how long this process will take, which is part of the challenge of holding the vision. There will be progress and breakthroughs, as well as setbacks and failures. All the drama of human life gets performed in the process of bringing a vision into reality no matter what its size or purpose.

Another important skill is to *hold* your vision in your mind's eye without allowing any of your own negative thoughts to have any effect. I like to surround my visions with a violet light of protection from all negativity.

Robert Scheinfeld, in his breakthrough book *Busting Loose from the Money Game,* describes the process by saying we all have our own quantum field that we use to create. He calls his visions "eggs." You put your egg in the quantum field and then protect it from any kind of negativity, especially your ego's habits of doubt, fear, and worry. With enough nurturing energy directed to the egg, eventually it will hatch.

Many books about the power of vision have been written, including one of my own titled *Trust Your Gut*. So there is lots you can read if this topic interests you. And I would like to mention a couple of additional concepts that will add major horsepower to your ability to manifest your vision.

One potent mental strategy is to *act as if your vision already exists*. It has been proven that your mind doesn't know the difference between something real and something imagined. It responds with equal intensity to both. So the more you imagine your vision to be real, the more your mind gets behind the idea and does its best to bring it into reality.

It's important to make sure your vision feels intuitively right. If the part of your mind that sees the big picture has decided that your vision has merit, fits your values, and feels like something you are supposed to do on a profound level, you have a keeper. You have to determine what feels right to you and no one else can do that for you.

Then taking it a step further, you can turn this vision into a mission or a purpose. In the Landmark Education vernacular, you "take a stand" for something that has meaning to you. You vow to do everything you can to bring this vision into reality regardless of the obstacles you may face.

In essence, you never give up. I like to add the qualifier that you never give up unless it feels intuitively right to do so. Sometimes there are things you need to give up. Only you can choose the worth of the vision and the commitment you make to it.

– *ACTION* –

Action, or *the act of doing,* is part two of the VAA Formula. Taking action is your goal with this book.

Taking action is the thing that has the biggest impact on the physical world. You get a response from the Universe when you take an action, things happen, people respond.

If you are trying to bring a vision into reality, you want to take the action that is most likely going to manifest your vision. In the case of prospecting, you need to make contact with a potential buyer of your product and make an offer. If you don't take this action, you are severely limiting your chances of success. Of course you can get lucky and have the stars align to create a miracle in your favor, but for now let's limit our discussion to the blood, sweat, and tears of doing the work.

One of the most powerful strategies I have found for taking action is to *commit to doing the required activities toward bringing your vision into reality.* This is such an obvious statement that I am embarrassed to admit that I have struggled with this issue.

There are things in life that seem to take more fortitude and commitment to do than others. Things like dieting, exercise, anything creative, anything involving personal growth or change, and, of course, prospecting. That's my list; I'm sure your list would have some variations. These kinds of activities have the potential for making us incredibly happy if we succeed, but are also prone to resistance, setbacks, and failure, which we would rather avoid.

So the more you can commit to doing the required activities toward your vision, the more success you are going to have. The problem is that for many of us, doing the required activities is simple but not always easy. It reminds me of a comment I got from a financial advisor I was talking to on the phone about coaching. He said, "I don't need a coach. I know exactly what I need to do. I just can't do it." I smiled and patiently explained to my prospect that finding a way to do the things you need to do is what a skilled coach can help you discover.

Another way to describe the right approach to taking action is to do what has to be done, not just what you *want* to do. I have spent too much time in my life thinking about doing things rather than just doing them. It felt like a good use of my time to try to figure out how to get rid of my resistance to doing what I need to do. Certainly some of the ideas I came up with were valuable and I'm sharing them with you in this book. But much of the time, my risk-averse ego was finding things for me to do that seemed more interesting or easier than prospecting and I paid dearly for that distraction.

One of the most important discoveries I have made about taking action is that it makes you *smarter*.

Something happens when you jump into the fray. Your mind wakes up, your body wakes up, the juices start to flow, and all of a sudden you have access to parts of your brain that were not there a second ago.

As you know by now, I am a big proponent of using the right side of the brain, which can process millions of pieces of information per second, as opposed to the left brain, which is exceedingly slow and plodding. When you are on the telephone making prospecting calls, or talking to people face-to-face, the more aware you are of your intuitive instincts the better. This is best described as trusting yourself to respond in the moment, in an appropriate way, without any prior knowledge of what you are going to say.

That may sound a little scary, but it's a skill you are going to want to develop. And it's easier than it sounds. You have to learn to hear the intuitive voice that we all have. Of course, parts of your opening language can be scripted, but the sooner you can move away from the script and have a real conversation with your prospect, the more likely something good will happen. Lots more on that topic ahead.

– ATTITUDE –

Attitude is the third part of the VAA Formula. Attitude is how you react to what happens when you take action toward your vision.

You have heard people say things like "Attitude is everything," or "Your attitude is your altitude." The state of mind you maintain in the face of challenge is a big factor in how fast you are going to make your vision a reality.

Ideally, you want to be learning from the results of the actions you take. Many find this a challenge if things are not going well. You assume that you are doing something wrong, or that there is something wrong with you. Once you engage a negative perspective, things usually go downhill quickly. The key is to see the positive value in whatever is happening. My mentor, Kurt, used to remind me that the Universe is teaching you how to succeed by the results you are getting if you pay attention.

The thing to be aware of is this: Are you learning to succeed from your results or are you letting your results beat you up?

One of my favorite quotes is from the writing of Mahatma Gandhi, "The secret to success is a burning passion and total detachment." How's that for simple and to the point? Burning passion equates to having a vision and taking action toward that vision. Total detachment is the key to maintaining a great attitude after you have taken action. If you don't care what other people think about you or what you are doing, you are not going to let anything stop you. You will find your way around the obstacles and eventually reach your goal.

I used to do a seminar titled *How to Get on a Roll and Stay on a Roll*. One of the key components was to learn not to judge whatever is happening, either good or bad. Simply do the next logical thing related to whatever you are trying to accomplish without any judgment.

If you are on the phone and you negatively judge what is happening, you will instantly become less effective and limit your options. It is also likely that your negativity will leak through into the conversation and your prospect will feel your angst and pull away.

The downside of getting too elated about something good happening is that it creates a strong contrast to the calls that are not as good, which creates a negative. I still like to pump my fist in the air after a good call, or extend my arms and hands up into the touchdown signal. It feels right to acknowledge the moment. But then I try to calm myself back down to a more Zen approach of seeing all the calls I make as important while being pleased with my ability to do my job.

Being solution-oriented is another excellent way to describe maintaining a positive attitude. If you are ruthlessly committed to finding a solution to whatever challenges you face, if you believe in your heart that there is an answer to whatever obstacle has presented itself, *you become a force of nature.*

There is always a moment of truth when you are faced with another obstacle or setback. How are you going to respond? Sometimes, you have worked hard, you are exhausted, and the bad news catches you off guard. You respond negatively. So far, not a problem. The trick is to quickly get back to a state of mind where you can best deal with the issue objectively without the negativity, and maybe even see if there is a lesson that can be learned.

The most exciting and fun aspect of the VAA Formula was Kurt's closing statement, which he would deliver with great delight. He would say, "If you follow this formula, only one of two things can happen. You are either going to get the result you are trying to create, or you will get a lesson required to get the result. *Therefore, you can't lose!*" I will always remember when I first heard Kurt say this with all the joy of his soul. I loved the idea that you can't lose no matter what happens, good or bad, success or failure.

– *LIGHTS, CAMERA, ACTION* –

So how do you apply the VAA Formula to your prospecting project?

You need a *vision* of yourself being successful. You have to define what that looks and feels like and in as much detail as you want. What values do you bring to the table? What are your interactions with your clients like? Who are your clients? What are they like: their values, their jobs, their personalities? Note anything else you want from your relationships. How does your success make you feel? What do you get to do because of your success? What influence do you have in the world?

Then you need some sales activity goals (*action*) to define how much of the required activities you need to do to reach your vision of success. (This approach works for dieting, exercise, and any other self-improvement endeavors.)

There are other ways to find clients besides calling them on the telephone. I get clients from the webinars I do, the books I have written, the extensive audio I have on the Internet, the referrals I ask for, and the unsolicited referrals I get from happy clients. You can add things like networking, direct mail, advertising, seminars, radio shows, etc.

Keep track of where your clients are coming from and the amount of time and money you are allocating to those sources.

Many of my coaching clients have done drip mailing campaigns of one form or another, or they send out newsletters every month. I ask them how many clients have come from that source. The answer often is, "None." If your answer is "None" or close to it, stop spending time, money, and energy on other people's good ideas and find the mix that works for you. The reality is that what works for someone else may not work for you.

You can make your record keeping as elaborate as you want. You can do amazing things with spreadsheet software, but most of my coaching clients tend not to get very excited about keeping track of a lot of numbers, so we decide on which ones are really important. Numbers like how much money do you want to make? What is the minimum you need and what is the upper end of what you would like to make? This creates a "range goal." You know what you need to make and you know what you want to make. Then you go for what you want.

When it comes to tracking telephone prospecting numbers, a couple of little tricks are helpful.

Keep track of numbers that demonstrate activity without requiring a positive response from the prospects you are calling. This helps minimize the ego's tendency to judge and evaluate your progress, which leads to a critical perspective that can "take the wind out of your sales." I keep track of how many times I dial the phone for this purpose. It keeps me in action doing the required activity of phoning without any judgment about how people are responding to my calls.

I like to remind myself that the most important thing I can do is to dial the phone. What happens after that is far less important.

The number of contacts you make is next. This also doesn't require any particular response from your prospects, but I do keep track of the positive responses. I keep numbers on who is interested in my work generally, which builds my email list, and who is interested in coaching which builds my inventory of potential clients. I keep spreadsheets on client inventory and client sales.

You will know within a few weeks of tracking your numbers how many of each number you need to create a client. Then you can set more realistic sales activity goals. The longer you track your numbers, the more accurately you will be able to predict the amount of prospecting activity required to make a sale.

Some sales cultures insist that keeping track of lots of different activity numbers is the key to success. But people are complicated and I think it's more important to find what works for you. I have coached many top advisors in the financial services industry. When you see how different they all are, you become less enamored with the conventional wisdom.

If you are one of those people who hates keeping track of numbers, keep it simple. In direct sales there are really only two numbers you need to monitor (and keep track of the names of your prospects): *How many people did you meet with? And how many of those people wrote you a check at some point?* A third number would be your vision of how much money you want to make. You can make your business plan that simple if you want.

The reason you keep track of numbers is to know how much sales activity you need to make a certain amount of money. There are plenty of successful people who don't keep track of any numbers other than the total of their paychecks.

Last but not least, let's do an *attitude* check.

What do you see when you look out into the future? Do you see the silhouettes of your clients, or is it a void? Do you wonder where your clients are going to come from again this year? The ego doesn't see very far ahead and tends to see only what is provable. The ego is afraid because it tends to see only what is not there! Your spirit can feel the presence of your clients. You may not be able to see their faces, but you can feel they are out there, they exist. To know in your heart that your clients are out there and your job is to find them, to find the right match, is the spirit-based approach to prospecting, on which I will go into greater detail in the next chapter.

– THE VISION BOARD –

Go to the office supply store and buy a piece of poster board or the matting used for picture framing.

Get on the Internet and find the best photos of the things you want to create in your life. You know: the things that give you a special feeling. They don't all have to be practical. It's okay to live a little or indulge feelings you don't totally understand.

One time I was looking through magazines for pictures I wanted to use on my vision board and saw an awesome photo of the Capitol in Washington, D.C. The picture moved me. I had a clear feeling that the Capitol was going to be part of my life somehow. I cut out the photo and put it on my board. Within a month I had a major speaking gig in Washington with a big new client I had no idea I could get.

There are a multitude of peel-and-stick stickers of every color and shape imaginable. Have some fun and create a visual way to keep track of your sales activity. I usually put the twelve months of the year down the side (or down the middle) and then put on a sticker to represent each of the new clients I want for that month. I write "John Doe" or "Jane Doe" on alternating stickers to represent that my clients already exist. Then I place a new, more colorful sticker on top of the old one when I get a client and write my new client's name on the sticker.

Use your imagination. You could have a different vision board for each month. You will also want to find an easy way to move your favorite photos from one board to another. You can measure any kind of sales activity you want. The most important thing is to have a vision of what you want to create and track your sales activity.

Remember, just because your analytical ego can't see who your clients are until they sign up that doesn't mean you can't generate an experience of the presence of those people. I'll make you a bet…that the more real you make the people you don't know or can't see yet, the faster they will show up.

THE VALUE OF WHAT YOU DO

You have to be convinced that what you are offering is of significant value to people. Or, the more you see the importance of what you are offering, the easier it is going to be to promote it.

Part of what you're offering is a product and part of it is *you*. Your values and the way you approach your work are a dominant factor in how others perceive the value of your proposition.

If you are new to prospecting, you do the best you can until you have more evidence and experience to back up your value. Until that time, you have to create a vision in your mind of people enjoying the benefits of your product and being better off because they met you. If you have experience, you can think about your best clients, your experience with them, how you helped them, and how thankful they were that you came into their lives.

When I start making prospecting calls, I take a few moments to think about the importance of what I am doing and the miracles that can happen for people when they find a way to take the action they want to take. The relationships I develop with clients are a great source of meaning and joy for me. I think of my favorite clients and imagine having ten more just like them. It makes it more worth the effort to prospect if I can see that the end result is new friends that I enjoy working with and helping them break through their barriers.

Another important consideration is that no one else can do the work I do exactly the way I do it. I am a perfect match for my clients, more than any other person. I imagine that my clients are out there waiting for me to call and that I need to initiate the process of finding them.

The reason it's so important to be convinced of the value of what you are offering is that you need to be a catalyst. You probably don't have a conglomerate spending millions of dollars to promote you and your product, so it's all up to you. *You* have to start the process of getting people's attention first, and then their interest, which creates the possibility for a sale to happen.

The idea of being a catalyst is important because it represents taking action, to get you to take the first step. Sometimes it helps to think about other ways you have taken the first step. Walking out onstage to give a talk is a good one. That is a performance of sorts, and making a prospecting call is a performance as well.

I was an expert snow skier at one point in my life and vividly remember pushing myself out of the starting gate as hard as I could at the sound of the starting buzzer. I played a lot of ice hockey when I was younger and often played the position of center. It's an exciting position because you start the play at the beginning of the game and after whistles. The centers are the two guys who face each other from opposing teams with their sticks about a foot apart to create a space for the referee to drop the puck, and that's when everybody jumps into action.

Star Trek: The Next Generation was a television show I enjoyed watching for years. A famous line from the show was by Captain Jean-Luc Picard. He said "Engage" while making a forward gesture with his arm and hand. His command informed the crew it was time to get the giant starship moving into action. In the most recent Star Trek movie, I noticed they now just say, "Punch it!" and the Starship jumps into warp speed. The visual is stunning.

So think of some of your own examples where you have been the catalyst and started something. It will help you remember the importance and power of prospecting, the first step of a sale.

We have talked about how the ego does not like prospecting and will usually attempt to find a reason for you not to make the call if you are not diligent in your awareness. In fact, if you don't fight your ego by coming up with reasons to call people, you will be no match for your ego's reasons not to call. When my ego is dreaming up reasons not to make calls, I have learned to counter them with thoughts like these:

• The reasons to make calls have to be bigger than the reasons not to.

- Be defiant about *making* calls instead of joining your ego and defiantly not making them.

- Find a reason to make the call, not a reason not to. Examples: *Why is this a great list of people to call now?* Or, *Why is this a perfect time to call this person?* Even a silly or fun reason to call someone works if it counteracts the ego's reason not to call: *This person doesn't know yet that my call will be one of the best parts of their day! I don't want to disappoint them!*

YOUR TEAM OF PERSONALITIES

There are a number of authors who have written books with some version of "Who's driving your bus?" in the title. I find the concept highly useful for our discussion of finding a way to get past the resistance to taking action.

We have been socialized to think we are crazy if we hear too many voices in our head or have multiple personalities. The reality is that having multiple personalities and hearing lots of different voices is more normal than not. In fact, the more creative you are, the more personalities you can access. The comedian and actor Robin Williams was a genius at giving life to all the personalities in his awareness in hilarious fashion.

We all have a whole team of personalities "sitting on our bus" doing their thing. And you get to choose whose driving the bus, who sits toward the front, and who sits in the back.

Here is a collection of some of the voices (personalities) in my head: Analytical Guy, Scared Guy, Skeptical Guy, Cautious Guy, Outgoing Guy, Resourceful Guy, Catalyst Guy, Improv Guy, Innovative Guy, Creative Guy, Powerful Guy, Fearless Guy, Unstoppable Guy, Intuitive Guy, Generous Guy, Loving Guy, Caring Guy, Empathetic Guy.

Can you guess who you want driving the bus and who should be part of the cheering squad surrounding your driver? It's not

Analytical Guy, Scared Guy, Cautious Guy, or Skeptical Guy.
And that's the team many would be prospecting masters have
at the front of their bus. No wonder they flounder.

You have to get the right guys or gals at the front of the bus.
You need Outgoing Guy, Fearless Guy, Resourceful Guy,
Intuitive Guy, and Caring Guy. And by all means, include
anyone else you think would be helpful in your case. I also
like to keep Playful Guy, Clever Guy, and Funny Guy around
for entertainment and to keep things on the lighter side. Some
of the guys on my bus are downright depressing.

When I am on the phone making prospecting calls, Outgoing
Guy and Resourceful Guy are doing all the heavy lifting. Then
I want to surround them with their best buddies, who will
cheer them on and not distract them or discourage them in any
way.

The Myers-Briggs personality test measures whether you are
an introvert or an extravert based on your responses to a series
of questions (*Please Understand Me* by David Kiersey and
Marilyn Bates). I score in the middle, which means I can go
either way, but I am much more comfortable being an
introvert. A couple of cocktails can help loosen things up, but
I don't recommend drinking and prospecting. So I have to
psych myself up to get on the phone. Sometimes I have to let
out a few loud Yee-Haws! like the cowboys do when they are
riding a bucking bronco. The louder I scream the better. Or a
quieter version is to do some stretches and throw ice-cold
water on your face.

I have to *act as if* I'm an extravert who has no fear of people
and can talk to anyone. Then I imagine my most outgoing self,
good on my feet while being friendly, warm, kind, patient,
loving, confident, generous, and generally a good guy who
cares about people and wants to help. I suspect most people
can make this adjustment if they have to.

You can do most anything for a short period of time if you can
find the right personality in your head. A true introvert is

probably never going to be comfortable making prospecting calls, but I have seen plenty of them do it.

If you can warm up the call with a referral or a good reason to call someone, that can be a big help for the more reserved folks. Susan Cain, in her groundbreaking book *Quiet*, says that one third of the population are introverts. So don't feel like the Lone Ranger if you need to have three lattes before you can find the nerve to get on the phone or just say hello to someone in a public place. I have days when I don't want to talk to anyone and skip the prospecting session that day. Most important is to commit to the prospecting activity numbers you need to reach your goals and then make them for the week or, for sure, for the month.

SUSPEND ALL NEGATIVE JUDGMENTS

Imagine for a minute what it would be like not to have any negative thoughts about anything. How would that make you feel? Your ego is going to have something to say about that, of course. Your ego is going to point out that with no negative experiences in your past you will have no idea what is dangerous and what to look out for and stay away from in order to avoid needless conflict.

I was having a conversation with a Landmark Forum trainer from Australia in a seminar I was attending in the Los Angeles center. (Landmark trainers are exceptional people. It takes seven years of rigorous training to be certified.) She made the point that if you have amnesia, you don't get upset. When I first heard her say that, I thought it was impossible. Then she went on to explain that with no past reference about what is upsetting, you are looking at everything newly for the first time. She was not saying that you couldn't get upset, just that the usual stuff that is upsetting to everyone else would not necessarily be upsetting to the person with amnesia. They have no memory of anything being upsetting!

A lightbulb went on in my head: I could use this concept for my coaching clients and my own struggles with making prospecting calls.

What if I could consciously create *negative prospecting experience amnesia?* Block out or suspend all my negative experiences with prospecting and anything else that my ego could use to stop me from taking action. I could foreseeably take away all my ego's power to hold me back.

Of course, your ego is going to think this is a ridiculous idea. What is your life going to be like without your ego looking out for you and keeping you out of danger? Your ego is going to make a passionate case for its job of protecting you. The bigger question is "Protect you from what?" Is prospecting inherently dangerous? No. Can you get physically hurt prospecting? No. Is someone going to come over to your office and rough you up because you called them during dinner? No. (But your ego is going to chime in with a warning, "But you never know…")

The reason the ego thinks prospecting is dangerous is that you are initiating a conversation that could lead to a negative response by another person. You are asking people to vote yes or no on your offer to help them. To the ego, the goal in life is to get everyone to like you and not upset anyone so you can survive. To the ego, prospecting isn't any less dangerous than being chased by a forty-foot-long Tyrannosaurus rex that wants to have you for a snack. (The T-rex could eat 500 pounds of another animal in one bite.)

So, can you see that the fears and doubts your ego has about you making prospecting calls or taking any kind of legitimate risk are unfounded? The ego is overreacting and being totally unrealistic. You are letting a tiny, overprotective part of your psyche determine the quality of your life. That really *is* nuts. That's way worse than having multiple personalities!

A number of powerful things happen with *Negative Prospecting Experience Amnesia* (I have now made that a real thing with capital letters, but not to worry: it's not a disease, it's a cure). You stop being afraid of what will happen when you make a call or take a risk. You stop being afraid of *what could happen* as well. You completely disengage your ego's ability to make up stuff to scare you and slow you down. Even your ego's ability to judge and evaluate whatever you are doing is given a death blow because it has nothing in the past to compare it to. Your ego can only watch what is happening for the first time just like you do and hope that everything turns out alright because it doesn't know what to do to stop you. Don't worry: your ego will still be coaching you every step of the way even though it has no clue.

The beautiful thing that happens with Negative Prospecting Experience Amnesia is that you block out all possible negative thoughts and can now dial into an ocean of possibility.

What is the opposite of *fear, doubt, worry, panic, anxiety,* and *fear of rejection? Trust* and *faith.* You have created an ideal state of mind to make calls from. There are no negatives, only trust and faith. You have nothing to be concerned about.

You simply make your calls, present your offer to people, and see what they have to say. It's what I call SW3—*Some will, some won't, so what.* Zig Ziglar gets credit for that one, even though it's my initials.

So now when you get on the phone, you have no fear of being judged by the other person. You expect to have a good call. Why wouldn't it be a good call? You are a good person, you want to help people, and you have a great product to offer those who are interested. If they do judge you or your offer, you simply notice that they are not interested or are in a bad mood and move on. It means nothing. You don't give the call another thought. The call that went nowhere doesn't matter at all in the grand scheme of things, which is the way it should be.

You have created a positive and powerful mental state for making prospecting calls where nothing bothers you. Guess how you keep this magical state of mind going?

You continue to create the experience of having Negative Prospecting Experience Amnesia. You keep the opening to your ideal prospecting mindset by eliminating the possibility of any negative judgment. Whatever happens, instead of judging and evaluating yourself and your performance, you look at whatever happens objectively and keep making calls. If it occurs to you to do something differently that you think might work better, you do that. You are naturally learning from your experience of making calls and naturally getting better with each call.

You might be saying this sounds really great and you would love to have this work, but you're not sure you know how to do the Negative Prospecting Experience Amnesia thing. Your ego is strong and smart and is making a great case for not picking up the phone. Okay, relax, take a deep, slow breath, and drop your energy down a few notches. You can do this.

Remember, you have more power than your ego. You are a chooser not a reactor, if you want to be. You get to choose what you think and feel about making calls. The most important thing to keep in mind is that your ego is like a little kid who is hungry and wants to be fed. You have to tell your ego that food is on the way, that the discomfort will only be for a few more minutes and things will be fine again. All the ego cares about is getting things back to normal, peaceful, no pending danger.

So you can say to your ego, "There is really no danger in making this call. It's okay if the person I'm calling is not interested." Let's talk more about that.

HOW TO DIFFUSE THE FEAR OF BEING JUDGED

Your ego makes you sensitive to being negatively judged. If you had a critical parent or if anyone important to you growing up was critical of you, your sensitivity to what you suspect others are thinking about you can be a hair trigger. Thinking that you are being negatively judged or criticized by someone can be perceived as a life or death situation to your ego, so the corresponding desire to get you to safety or fight back can be extreme.

The fighting-back option is usually not one that we use in relation to prospecting. The ego's main goal is to keep us from making calls rather than fighting with people who judge you. However, if you have a sensitivity to being judged, you can easily find yourself yelling at someone on the phone to give them a piece of your mind. Or you may feel totally justified in being mean toward them if you feel frustrated or if you are treated unfairly or not respected. To fight back by being negatively critical, sarcastic, demanding, or demeaning to the person on the other end of the line can make you feel good temporarily, but you will feel the effects of such a negative response if you are sensitive toward people.

The same applies to getting angry; nothing good will ever come from that. The rush of anger can make you feel like you won the battle momentarily, but the negative fallout is usually that you eventually feel bad and wish you hadn't gotten angry in the first place. *Just say no* to fighting back.

The fear of being negatively judged has given me the most trouble. I had a negative parent who made me think whatever I did was never good enough. I have coached many people with the same issue. The most important thing is to recognize these negative thoughts and see them for what they are, a replay of old experiences that have little or nothing to do with what is currently happening. I will admit that this enlightened point of view can take some practice.

Let's take an objective look at what is actually happening when someone is saying no to you.

The most obvious conclusion is that they are simply not interested in your offer. It doesn't mean that they have any negative feelings toward you or that they are questioning your value or your ability to do your job. They may already have someone in their life taking care of whatever you are offering. Or they may have made a decision not to deal with the issue you are representing.

There are any number of logical reasons for someone not to be interested in the offer you are making. It's like walking into a large retail store. The number of items you are not interested in for a variety of reasons is substantial. You may not have an interest in *anything* in the store even when there are thousands of items. So the first thing you have to consider is that it is totally logical and okay if people are not interested in your offer. It means absolutely nothing and is of no consequence.

Next you have to consider that someone's lack of interest does not have an underlying message that questions your skill level or ability to do your job. If someone said they were "not interested" when I first got into sales, I assumed it meant either that there was something wrong with my pitch or the way I said it, or that they thought I somehow did not know what I was doing. I spent endless hours trying to fix all those issues and be ready for the next caller who had no interest. This was a lot of work and didn't really help that much. I struggled for many years before I learned that when someone is not interested in my offer, it is not a reflection on me in any way.

I finally learned that I didn't need to change my phone approach every time someone wasn't interested. Really, I actually used to do that. I was so analytical and naive, I thought that if someone can say no to my great offer, I must be doing it wrong or need to change the offer. I don't do that anymore.

Of course, there are times when you get someone on the phone who is having a bad day or just plain mean and gives you a hard time. Those are not people you want as clients anyway. I didn't know that for a long time and would try to have conversations with toxic people because I thought my job was to talk them into an appointment no matter what. I was taught that not getting an appointment was a failure. You can feel verbally beat up trying to get negative people to want to do something positive. I eventually learned that people lashing out at me was more about them than about me.

Now that I understand more about why people are negative, I realize they are having a difficult time. I actually now have some compassion for those people. The reality is that people are doing the best they know how to do, even if what they are doing is idiotic. Furthermore, I have been there, totally stuck and frustrated in my negativity, trying to do everything I know to do but it isn't working. Nothing works with a negative attitude.

I don't spend time on the phone with the negative types anymore, but I acknowledge their pain. I would not want to be them for a minute and have that horrible attitude. Also, since I am so sensitive to other people's negative judgment, if I feel the knife approaching my abdominal area, I realize it is insane to stay on the phone and be verbally abused. That doesn't happen very often, but it *can* happen.

It is more important to protect my attitude during my phoning session than it is to accommodate people with a bad attitude. Also, it is far better to retreat than to fight back if you get emotionally triggered.

If I sense someone has an attitude issue, I will get off the phone as quickly as possible or simply hang up. Sometimes I decide not to talk to people because of how they answer the phone. If the energy is too negative, I just say, "I'm sorry, I must have the wrong number." If I am farther in to my pitch, I may just say, "I don't think I can help you. Good luck to you." And then hang up.

An empowering paradigm shift is to make it a win when someone is not interested. Making the call that goes nowhere is just as important as the great call. Your narrow-minded ego will argue with this logic, but if you shift to a bigger perspective, you realize the duds are required to succeed. Why not give all calls equal significance no matter what happens? The more you can learn not to judge the people who judge you, the happier and more successful you will be. I would go as far as to say it is a guarantee of your success if you are not affected by other people's responses to you or your offer.

Just remember that how people respond to you is more about them than you. It doesn't matter how they respond. If you make enough calls, you are going to get winners. When I was doing service with monks in a monastery in Long Beach during my free time, which I did for ten years, they had a simple saying that sums up this perspective: *"If you judge, you lose."*

BREAKTHROUGH NO EXPERIENCE

There is an exercise I developed years ago that has been helpful to many people.

I call it the *Breakthrough No Experience*. You will need a partner and a script of potential questions to ask. Read requests or pitches or offers to your partner and have them say no to you in whatever form occurs to them. Part of their job is to be creative with how they say no, although the exercise works even if your partner is not particularly creative.

Another version of the exercise is to alternate between a yes and a no to your offer, which some say is more realistic and less in-your-face. But I recommend you do ten no responses in a row to get in touch with how you react when you hear a no. After the initial ten no's, your partner can decide which offers they want to say yes or no to and how many yeses or no's they do in a row. You make the offer, your partner responds yes or no, and *then you experience whatever you feel.*

The goal is to get to the point where you lose your panic and negative visions if someone says no to you. Once you get to the experience where a no response is okay with you, you have had the Breakthrough No Experience.

You are A, and your partner is B. Here is how it goes...

A: "I'd like to talk to you about our new vitamin program for better health."
B: "No. I don't want to talk about that."

A: "Would you like to go with Mary and me to have lunch?"
B. "No."

A: "Why not?"
B: "I don't want to talk about it."

A: Can I ask you for a favor?"
B. "No."

A. "Are you happy with what you are doing with your money?"
B. "No."

A. "If I could help you do better with your money, would that be of interest to you?
B: "No."

A. "Do you like to send out greeting cards?"
B. "Yes."

A. "I'd like to show you some really neat greeting cards."
B. "Okay."

A. "I'd like to take you to dinner."
B. "No."

A. "Can I ask why?"
B. "Yes, you can ask, but I'm not going to tell you why."

It helps to create a list of questions before you start. You can improvise and wander off script; just keep asking questions your partner can say yes or no to. Remember, your objective as participant A is to feel how you respond to no and see if you can experience having it not matter whether people say yes or no.

Don't make this exercise too serious and significant. Have fun with it. Just having someone say no to you ten times in a role-play can break you through to new levels of composure and detachment toward other people judging you.

Ideally, you want to be able to face the unknown of how people will respond to you when you ask them a yes or no question. That is what you are doing when you prospect. At some point in the conversation you offer something they can say yes or no to and that creates all the problems as well as the opportunities. When you get to the point that you can stay present and resourceful regardless of how people respond to you, you will begin to feel like you can handle anyone on the phone or anywhere else. Now you are finding the *zone* or a *resource state* where you are unstoppable, which is our next topic.

THE RESOURCE STATE

Early in my career, I studied to be a Neuro-Linguistic Programming (NLP) practitioner. I found the course material fascinating and learned a lot about how the brain works, but it didn't fit my intuitive coaching style. After completing the course work, I decided that I liked using my intuition more than the NLP techniques. I thought the material was excellent, it just wasn't how I wanted to coach. However, one of the concepts I found useful for overcoming fear and resistance was creating a *resource state*.

The idea of a resource state is that you can define what you're like when you are at your best. You can create an experience of that state and bring it into being *on command,* so to speak.

For example, if I am getting ready to walk out onstage and give a talk, I will do better if I am in touch with the feeling of me being at my best in front of an audience, which is the resource state. You can use this technique in a wide variety of settings. I have a resource state for when I coach, when I write, when I play tennis, when I dance. You can create a resource state for anything.

There are a variety of ways to create a resource state. I will give you three different approaches. Some work better than others for different people. You have to experiment to find what works best for you.

I have gotten value from all three of the NLP approaches and have created many other versions of the resource state. You could say this whole book is about creating a resource state for you to take action toward doing the things you need to do.

1. One of the ways to create a resource state is to identify the qualities you want to feel and then anchor that feeling to a spot on your hand like a knuckle. Read all the qualities you want to feel before you walk out on stage to give your talk. Get the experience as clearly in your mind and feelings as possible, the feeling of what you are like at your very best onstage, and then touch the knuckle below your left index finger. The idea is that if you have created a strong enough anchor feeling of your resource state, you can then just touch your anchor knuckle as you walk out onstage and you are instantly in that feeling of you at your best.

Some of the students in my NLP class swore by that procedure, most of whom were women. It never worked for me that well. I assumed it was because I am more visual and auditory and less kinesthetic. I feel things, but I am not particularly in touch with what is going on in my body as some people are. So I would guess this approach is better for those who are more kinesthetic. I am also the first to say that people are complex and you never know what is going to work for you. So experiment and see what happens.

2. The second approach to creating a resource state is called the *Circle of Excellence*. Draw a circle on the floor with chalk or create a circle some other way about three feet in diameter. Then take your list of the qualities of you being at your best and imagine them being in that circle. So, when you step into that circle, you become all of your best qualities for whatever activity you want to perform. The anchor is the circle in this case. I found it useful to imagine a circle around the podium where I would be speaking and then step into that circle as I began my talk. Obviously, there are lots of ways to create the experience of being at your best. These are little games you can play to get you headed in the right direction.

3. The most interesting experience for me is called the *Squash Technique*. Again, there are a variety of ways to do this exercise, but I would do it with my hands. Take your left hand and imagine a version of yourself in as much detail as possible before you became a good speaker. Then in your right hand, imagine a version of yourself at your best as a speaker—again, in as much detail as possible. Then when you have a clear impression of both of these people, put your hands together and hold for ten seconds. Often when I did this exercise I would feel things that I could not describe, but it always seemed to work. I always felt more confident and my talks went well.

Now that you understand the concept of creating a resource state, you can get even more creative.

My favorite resource state for telephone prospecting is what I call the *Cone Zone*. You remember the old TV show, *Get Smart*? It was a spy spoof starring Don Adams as Maxwell Smart and Barbara Feldon as Agent 99. There was a scene in the show when they wanted to have a super-private conversation that no one else could possibly hear. After all, they were sharing top secrets. To facilitate the experience of total privacy, they would lower the *Cone of Silence,* which was a giant Plexiglas cone that was totally soundproof. Of course, you could read their lips and see the expressions on their faces, but that didn't seem to be of any concern to anyone, which made it even funnier.

So for me to get into my Cone Zone is to visualize a giant cone coming down over my head as I get ready to make prospecting calls. Except that the function of my cone is not to create privacy but to block out all negative thoughts. I have even added my *Negative Prospecting Experience Amnesia* to the mix. So when I bring the cone down over my head, I am protected from all negative thoughts and have no memory of any negative prospecting experiences from the past. Pretty cool, eh? (I grew up near the Canadian border north of Detroit, so I say "Eh" once in a while.)

In my self-created Cone Zone, my own negativity can't touch me. Other people's negativity can't touch me. I am totally protected! Obviously, these are mental tricks to get you to focus on what you want to create and not be distracted by your own negative thoughts. It's also a way to make doing something challenging more fun which I have always found to be effective. If you can smile while you're on the phone, you are going to do better.

THE SPORTS ANALOGY

You have heard the saying "Sports is life." There would not be the fascination with sports if it was not a direct reflection of life. As it turns out, sports is analogous to many of the points I am making in this book.

I have many highly skilled golfers as coaching clients. They are all financial advisors who use golf as a method of establishing relationships with potential well-heeled clients. In a typical golf match, you spend several hours together with three other people with lots of time to talk and see how everyone responds under pressure.

One of my advisor clients used to play on the PGA and we spent hours preparing him before matches. A profound skill for a golfer is to stay focused on the big picture. When you stand up to address the ball, you don't want to be using your analytical mind and its narrow focus. That's the best way to hit the ball in the woods.

Your focus needs to be on a vision of the perfect shot and/or the feel of that shot as you hit it. Then you step up to the ball and without thinking hit the shot you saw and felt. If you let your analytical mind into the picture, you will be distracted from your ideal focus and unable to hit the shot you envisioned. Your analytical mind cannot hit a golf shot other than by sheer luck. It will try to convince you otherwise, and it will be quick to offer you advice and reasons why you just hit such a poor shot. The reality is that the body movement of a golf shot is way too complicated for the analytical mind to comprehend.

I have spent many hours playing tennis with pros, taking lessons and fine-tuning my game. My serve is above average because of one simple thing. I have disciplined myself not to look to see whether I hit a good serve until after the ball has crossed the net. There is a reason for this. If I let my controlling ego look to see how I did before I completed my serve, it would drop my shoulder by an eighth of an inch and my serve would hit the tape on the top of the net. I can do this ten times in a row and hit the exact same spot on the net each time. It's amazing to watch.

My intuition (right brain) knows exactly where the lines are on the tennis court. I don't have to look. My analytical ego wants to look to see how I did because it has no trust or faith in my intuitive ability. As one of my tennis coaches put it, if you want to be really good at serving, you don't get to see the serve. But you will know if the serve was good. You will learn what it feels like when the serve is good without looking, and you will also observe your opponent scrambling to hit it back. Often without success.

Baseball is probably the best analogy for making prospecting calls because there are so many similarities. In prospecting, you can be successful with a high failure rate just as in baseball. The best baseball players are hitting fair only around 30 percent of the time. A batting average of .330 is rare with only thirty players hitting that mark. Ty Cobb holds the record for the best batting average at .366. That means the rest of the best players have at least a 70 percent failure rate.

Prospecting is similar. A 20 to 30 percent success rate on the phone is excellent. You can make a living with a 10 percent success rate, which means you are failing 90 percent of the time. It takes a special kind of mental focus to fail nine times out of ten and be able to keep going.

In baseball, the required activity is to hit a fair ball. If you don't swing, you can't get a hit. You swing at the pitches that you feel you can hit. Or you can be like Babe Ruth and swing as hard as you can at almost every pitch. We all know the batting record of the Great Bambino. He found an approach that worked for him. Of course, you can get on base if you are pitched four balls and are walked. But you can't make a living with this approach because the odds are against you getting more balls than strikes. Plus, no one would want to watch such a boring game and you would be fired. Similarly, if you don't prospect, odds are you will be fired as well. For sure, you will find it difficult to make any money.

Baseball is also an excellent analogy for people who are struggling with prospecting. When people make their calls and get discouraged at the number of no's, I say you have to approach it the same way you play baseball. If you strike out, how do you feel? Do you feel like quitting and never playing again, or are you excited to get up to bat to see if you can do better next time?

What is the difference between prospecting and playing baseball? For most of us, it's money. We play baseball for fun not for money, so there is nothing to lose. If you can prospect with the attitude that you have nothing to lose, and you can't wait to get up to bat again after you strike out, you are going to do well at prospecting.

In the Landmark Education Forum training, they talk about the choice of being a player on the court or an observer in the stands. The observer is safe in the stands, with no risk and no potential embarrassment of failure. But you can't win the game or anything else in the stands. You have nothing at stake. You are not playing to win; you are watching others compete. Which quality do you want to have in your own life? Do you want the thrill of victory? Or do you want to hang out and watch others do battle and live your life by watching others struggle with theirs? To put yourself in the game where you can lose or fail takes guts. You are going to be rejected, challenged, frustrated, and generally pushed to your limits.

But there is one thing you get being in the game that you can't get in the stands. Of course, you get to experience winning, but you don't win all the time. It's bigger than that. You get to experience having success even though you may be unsuccessful much of the time.

Putting the effort into prospecting has that kind of reward. Even if you are failing 70 percent of the time with your prospecting, you are going to do well with the 30 percent who respond positively. Years ago I got out my calculator and determined that Ken Griffey Jr., who was playing for the Seattle Mariners, made $50,000 every time he hit the ball and got on base or hit a home run. That's good pay for a 70 percent failure rate.

THE DICE GAME

The idea of the dice game came to me many years ago as a way to create some audience participation when I was speaking. My goal was to demonstrate to the audience how to shift to a bigger perspective and anchor the experience with something fun and colorful that involved movement, made noise, and got some laughs.

I would give each audience member a pair of dice and say we were going to roll the dice ten times. Each roll of the dice was the same as making one prospecting call. I would then instruct the audience that before they rolled the dice, I would give them a reason not to make the call from their analytical ego. Then do three things:

1. Repeat the reason not to make the call out loud.

2. Roll the dice. If they got a seven, eleven or doubles, that was an appointment. Anything else was a failed call.

3. Record whether they got an appointment or not on each call.

We would then proceed with the exercise, which was loud, chaotic, and great fun. Can you imagine a couple hundred people repeating reasons not to make prospecting calls and then having them all roll their dice? Some audience members became very excited and expressive when they got an appointment! At the completion of the exercise, we would determine who got the most appointments and I would give out prizes to the winners.

So, you get the general idea of how this would work in front of an audience. Instead of reading the exercise the way I would do it when I speak, I'm going to give you an even more creative version, which is an excerpt from my new novel.

The LightSpace Ultimatum: Evolve or Die is my most creative endeavor. I wanted to see if I could write an engaging story and include some of my most profound peak performance discoveries. The novel is an action-adventure love story with a sci-fi twist, and embedded in the story are important lessons for overcoming your greatest fears.

Our hero, Luke, has loads of latent talent, but his resistance is holding him back, until he meets Sophia, a mystery woman he can't resist. She needs his help to save the world and singles him out for a special kind of training, starting with showing him how to conquer his call reluctance.

There is a description of the novel on Amazon, so I am not going to discuss any further details here. However, let me set the scene. Sophia is a brilliant sales coach (late twenties) teaching Luke how to overcome his fear of making prospecting calls. Luke, also in his late twenties, is a somewhat successful financial advisor. They are making calls from his apartment in Venice Beach, California, with a view of the Pacific off in the distance.

– The Tale of Luke & Sophia –

"I still like hanging out with you more than I enjoy making sales calls," said Luke.

"It's your lucky day, you get to do both," said Sophia.

"I wish I had as much confidence in me as you do."

"Don't worry, you don't need confidence, you need guts. And you have the guts of a burglar. You let your worries keep you from making calls, and I have to show you how to stop that. Which, if I understand correctly, is something you want to learn how to do."

"You are great, you are wise," I said with a bow.

"That's good. You keep that sense of humor around when you're making calls and you'll have no trouble at all. Who was the worrier when you were growing up?"

"My mother. She thought her job in life was to worry about her children, and everything else for that matter."

"A lot of people think that worrying helps somehow," she said. "It doesn't! Worrying is a form of negative thinking that is our biggest enemy in the fight for lightspace. Under pressure, most people create a negative vision of what *could* happen. Then they worry about the negative vision they created. That is not a resourceful state for living your life."

"So it's a war against negativity," I said.

"That's the battle. There are people who think it's positive to worry about all the things that *could* go wrong and keep track of what they did wrong so they don't do it again. But if you're focused on the negative, guess what you create more of?"

"The negative."

"If you say to yourself, 'Don't be afraid of the phone,' what does your mind have to do first?"

"Think about being afraid of the phone."

"Right. Then what's step two?"

"Try not to be afraid of the phone."

"It doesn't work. The message to your brain is *be afraid of the phone*," she said.

"So how do we kill off the *fear of the phone monster* once and for all?"

"We have to get the right guys in your head at the front of the bus."

"Which guys do you want?" I asked.

"Gutsy Guy, Intuitive Guy, Resourceful Guy and Outgoing Guy for sure."

"Who do you want me to move to the back?"

"Scared Guy, Analytical Guy, Worried Guy and Skeptical Guy. Let's move them to the back of the bus and let them watch movies about the end of the world."

I chuckled at the irony. "I feel better already."

"That's a good sign. All right, I have a present for you. Close your eyes and give me your hand."

"That reminds me of a couple jokes."

"Stay with me now. No time to travel back to the fraternity house. Close your eyes." She put something square with sharp edges in my hand and then closed my hand. There were two of them. "Keep your eyes closed for a minute. I'm not done with this part yet."

"I think I can guess what they are!" I sounded like a little kid.

"Shhh! Let me finish my ceremony." She gently placed both of her hands around my hand. "These are special dice that will always remind you that *if you keep rolling the dice, you will roll a winner*. The only way you can lose is to stop rolling the dice. I want you to feel my love in these dice and my love for you as a partner in the most important mission in history."

"Thanks. That means a lot."

The energy this beauty could generate would light up a small city. Combine that with her pure love and you were ready to move mountains.

"Open your eyes," she said.

There were two large crystal-clear red dice with white dots. The casino name was stamped in a circle around each snake eye.

"I have given you two registered dice from the Hard Rock Casino in Las Vegas. They have actually been rolled on the roulette tables there at least once. More important is for you to be aware of the energy I have given them."

"I'll remember."

"Okay, Romeo, let's do a warm-up for getting you on the phone. Here's how it works. I say a reason not to make a call. Then you repeat the reason out loud after me and then roll your dice. Sevens, elevens and doubles are appointments. Anything else is a call that didn't go anywhere. You roll ten times. Write down how many appointments you get. Got it?"

"Let's do it," I said.

"Number one. Repeat after me: 'I don't feel like prospecting today.' Then roll the dice."

"Okay. 'I don't feel like prospecting today.' Seven! Got my first appointment."

"Did anyone ever call you *dumb luck?*" she said. "Number two: 'It never seems like the right time to call.'"

"'It never seems like the right time to call.' Five. No appointment, darn."

"Number three: 'This person is probably already working with a financial advisor.'"

"'This person is probably already working with a financial advisor.' Doubles, two threes, appointment!"

"That's good, two out of three," she said. "Number four: 'I'm not sure what to say to this person.'"

"'I'm not sure what to say to this person.' Nine. Boo..."

"Number five: 'I can make these calls tomorrow.'"

"'I can make these calls tomorrow.' Eleven, appointment!"

"You know the most significant thing about tomorrow?" she asked.

"What's that?"

"Tomorrow never comes. Number six: 'I don't have time to prospect.'"

"'I don't have time to prospect.' A three plus one is four. Shoot!"

"Now let me ask you an important question," she said. "Do the dice care what you are thinking before you roll them?"

"No."

"Does what you are thinking have any effect on the dice?"

"Probably not. No."

"Precisely. The dice do their own thing regardless of what you are thinking. Number seven: 'Prospecting takes too much time.'"

"'Prospecting takes too much time.' Three plus five is eight. Foiled again!"

"Number eight: Fill in the blank, 'I would rather be...'"

"'I would rather be saving the world with Sophia.' Eleven, appointment!"

"I like your answer," she said. "Number nine: A special one for you innovators and rebels, 'There has to be an easier way!'"

"'There has to be an easier way!' I like that one," I said. "Six and four. Another dog."

"And last, number ten: For the experienced advisor like yourself, 'I've paid my dues. I shouldn't have to make these calls!'"

"'I've paid my dues. I shouldn't have to make these calls!' Snake eyes! All right!"

"Count up your appointments," she said.

"Five out of ten."

"How do you feel about that?"

"If I can get five out of ten appointments, they'll be talking about me around the water cooler!"

"How many appointments you got isn't what's important, however. Let me ask you a couple more questions to make my point. Can you roll the dice correctly?" she asked.

"No. You might think you can, but not really."

"Can you control the dice?"

"No. Not really."

"Does it matter what you think of before you roll the dice?"

"No."

"Can you get an appointment if you don't roll?"

"No."

"So what conclusion would you make from this exercise?" she asked.

"The most important thing is to roll the dice. *If you don't roll, there is no possibility for success.*"

"Your hockey brother Wayne Gretzky said something like 'You miss 100 percent of the shots you don't take.'"

"He did say that. I'm impressed."

"Do you know how these people are going to respond before you make the call?"

"No idea," I said.

"So do you hear what you're saying? You have no idea how people are going to respond until you make the call! So where do your fears, doubts, worries and other concerns come from?"

"Past experience?" Seemed like the right answer to me.

"Correct! Do they have anything at all to do with the call you are about to make?"

"No. It's a totally new call."

"That's the opening or window where you can make calls with no resistance. Do you get it? Can you see it? Can you feel it?"

"Yeah, the window is making calls without remembering any past experience to make you afraid or anxious," I said.

"That's it. If you had amnesia and couldn't remember any of your past prospecting calls, would you have any call reluctance?"

"No."

"No is right. You would have no reference point to make you worried or fearful or negative in any way. What do you suppose is next?"

"To make calls?" I said tentatively.

"Good answer. We also need to keep you in good shape by controlling the quality of your calls. Have you ever had calls not go very well?" she asked.

"Sure."

"How did that make you feel?"

"Lousy."

"What went wrong or what didn't work?" she asked.

"It's usually because the other guy gives you a hard time."

"So not very friendly."

"Not at all."

"How do the calls go if the other person is friendly?" she said.

"Usually pretty good. I may not get an appointment but it's a decent experience."

"So here's rule #3. Don't talk to anyone who's giving you a hard time or who's in a lousy mood."

"How do I do that?"

"It's easy. You just push any three numbers." She pressed three numbers on the phone. "Then hang up. They think something went wrong with the phone when they hear the three beep tones. That gives you a way out. They're glad to be off the phone and they won't call back."

"So if I don't like what's happening on the call, I push three buttons and bail."

"That's rule #3. Stay in a good mood. Enjoy making calls. Have fun making calls. If you get an attitude on the other end, you bail. You don't let civilians with a bad attitude bring your vibration down."

"I feel like a moron for asking, but what's Rule #1 and #2?"

"Rule #1 is: *You can't make an appointment without rolling the dice!* Rule #2 is: *Isolate yourself from your past and you have no fear.*"

"I knew that," I said. Having fun with Sophia made this discussion tolerable. I was trying to ignore the fact that I could be making a total fool of myself in front of her at any moment.

"Do you have your script and some prospects to call?" she asked.

"I do."

"What are you feeling?"

"Nervous, excited. A little concerned that the guy on the other end might yell at me and tell me to go to you-know-where. Other than that, I'm having a great time."

"Let's do this. Dial your first number," she said.

* * * * * *

After overcoming his call reluctance, Luke discovers he has to face much more daunting obstacles. He learns from Sophia

75

that Earth is about to be destroyed, but humanity has one last chance to save itself. Sophia recruits Luke to be part of an elite group of people who are being trained by extraterrestrials to achieve an enlightened mental state called *lightspace*, but it may be too late!

You'll have to read the novel to find out what happens. My coaching clients who have read the novel say they loved the book and that it was a fun and entertaining way to learn important lessons about overcoming fear and resistance.

You can get *The LightSpace Ultimatum: Evolve or Die,* at Amazon.com.

YELLOW PAD PATROL

When I get ready to make prospecting calls, I always have a yellow pad within easy reach. I like to listen to what the voices in my head are saying. If I hear a negative phrase or thought, I write it down on the yellow pad. I will do this sometimes while the phone is ringing after I dialed the number I was calling. I find this can take away any nervous energy I may have about whoever I'm calling. It feels risky and gutsy to be thinking about something else besides just what I'm going to say when the person answers. It's a show of confidence and I like the feeling.

So I write down the negative thought on the yellow pad and then look for its counterpart from a bigger perspective. Let's say I have the feeling that I don't want to make these calls because I am remembering what it feels like to be rejected. I open myself up to my army of information from the bigger perspective and listen. Then I write down what pops into my head:

• Lack of interest is not a rejection. It's okay if people are not interested in my offer. I am looking for people who *are* interested. You have to have one to have the other in this reality.

• I make money with each dial, not by people's response.

• I don't have to sell anybody. I am looking for people who are open to what I have to offer. If they are not open to me, I get off the call and on to the next one.

• I have no idea how people are going to respond until I make the call. This next call could be my next client. Remember, it's like getting up to bat after you strike out. Go for it! Don't shy away…swing for the fence!

You get the idea. I am shifting from the fearful, doubtful, scared, whining voice of my analytical ego trying to keep me off the phone to the bigger perspective of my fearless, intuitive spirit, which has the whole Universe as a support team.

There are over 180 phrases and one-liners from the bigger perspective to counteract your ego-based fearful, doubtful thoughts in Chapter 8. Your ego won't stand a chance!

One final thought on this topic. You don't have a lot of time to make these mental shifts when you are phoning because you need to respond when someone answers on the other end. But you don't need more than a second to hear what's going on in your head and find a positive response from a bigger perspective. The pressure of continuing to make calls will make your insights more powerful. It won't be long before you have favorite paradigm shifters that will keep you in the zone.

I said earlier that being in action makes you smarter. I can readily say that many of my most valuable insights related to overcoming my fears and resistance have come from the Yellow Pad Patrol.

Keep track of your notes. When you get a few pages, type them up in a word processing document for safekeeping and future reference. My "Calling Notes" were the main source for this book.

6. THE SPIRIT-BASED APPROACH

YOUR SPIRIT IS ALIVE

It will be no surprise that a theme in my life is moving from being a controlling, survival-oriented ego to being a flowing, all-knowing, intuitive spirit. I try not to use the word *spiritual* because it pulls in all kinds of past experience that has been intellectualized by the analytical ego. The ego can't intellectualize your actual spirit. *Your spirit is alive. Your spirit lives in the present moment. Your spirit is the chooser of what you experience in life.* Your spirit is the real you, the self with a capital S, or *Self.* Some would call your spirit your Higher Self, or God Self. Some might say it is the part of you that is somehow connected to God or whoever you believe the Higher Power to be.

Your spirit is big, undefined, and greatly unknown. You can feel your spirit. You can recognize its presence. You can see its influence. But you can't see your spirit. One of the words I like to use to describe your spirit is *mystical. Mystical* means transcending human understanding, inspiring a sense of mystery, awe, fascination; concerned with soul or spirit rather than with material things; unseen, unexplained, uncontrolled by the ego, beyond the limitations of the intellect and observable proof.

Is it possible that your spirit is who you are being when you're not being your ego? That is an oversimplification, but it works for our discussion. You need to define as best you can who you are if you are not being your ego. This approach gives you two contrasting choices that are easily identified. You are using either the e*go-based approach* or the s*pirit-based approach*.

We have been progressively defining the ego-based approach in previous chapters. This chapter is about defining the spirit-based approach, or at least showing you what it looks like in action when you are prospecting or doing anything you need to do.

See the table in the Appendix titled *The Qualities of Ego VS. Spirit.*

MYSTICAL MOMENTUM

When you dial the phone or take any action that would be considered prospecting, you are stirring the energy of the Universe in your favor. We are all miniature creators. So when you take action with a conviction about the offer you are extending to improve someone's life in some way, there is a reaction in the world. I call it m*ystical momentum*. If you stir up the energy in the Universe enough, the powers that be say, "Okay, she is making an effort. Give her a reward!" and you experience some success.

You never know precisely where your success is going to come from. It's not uncommon that success will come from somewhere other than the prospecting calls you are currently making. What I find in my own practice is that if I consistently make prospecting calls, it seems to push new clients in the door. People magically fall off the fence of indecision and decide to hire me. Or the phone rings with a potential client who found me on the Internet.

It would be difficult to prove the existence of mystical momentum, but you can see its impact. Let's put it this way: when I don't prospect consistently, my negative thoughts about *not* prospecting take their toll and the momentum fades. Of course, there are other ways to prospect and promote yourself besides making direct calls. I have found making direct prospecting calls to be a powerful way to create mystical momentum and it is much simpler than the many other forms of prospecting and promotion.

Another way to explore the idea of mystical momentum is to ask yourself these questions:

• What if you are given clients for a whole different set of reasons than the ones you think you understand?

• What if you are actually given clients because of how much of the right effort you put forth and who you are being when you call?

• What if you are supposed to be helping people make an informed decision more than trying to talk them into something?

• What if the way people respond to you is really out of your control?

• What if the idea that you are causing the sale to happen is an illusion?

Absolutely, you are an important part of the process, but maybe not in the way you have been trained to think. My experience is that I make more sales and feel better about myself when I help people decide what feels right to them than when I try to talk them into buying. That is the essence of the Relationship Builder approach to sales and self-promotion as described in Chapter 4. It's also a clear expression of the spirit-based approach because you are being more of a spirit and less of an ego when you help people decide what they really want.

GOD'S SELECTION PROCESS

This is a good place to introduce a powerful premise that I call *God's Selection Process*. The idea behind God's Selection Process is that God gets to decide who your clients are going to be, not you. Your job is to initiate the process, be at your best throughout the process, and trust the results. God actually needs you to make the calls so you can find the right clients. In this way of thinking, prospecting starts the selection process.

In this dualistic reality, in order to have success, there has to be failure by contrast. In prospecting, in order to have the right match, you have to have situations that are *not* the right match. Without the contrast, there is no game to play.

Werner Erhard, a brilliant mentor used to say, *"In order to have a game, what you don't have has to be more important than what you've got."* In this case, you want clients who you don't have yet, so there's a game to play. In order for a game to be interesting, there have to be winners and losers. Would you watch professional athletes compete with no scoreboard and no time clock? It might be interesting for a while, but it would eventually get boring with nothing at stake.

One of the keys to embracing God's Selection Process is to rise above the ego's need to constantly judge and evaluate how you are doing. It doesn't matter if you are winning or losing. All that's required of you to engage God's Selection Process is that you show up and play the game.

I read something recently that had a profound impact on me: "The most successful people are the ones who fail the most."

It's not like I had never heard this idea before. There are many famous examples like Thomas Edison and the lightbulb. But what I realized was that somewhere in the back of my mind, I had decided that failure was bad and that I should avoid it as much as possible. Makes sense, right? Yes, it makes sense to your ego which is trying to control the results and not fail. But to my intuitive spirit doing God's Selection Process, failure is not a bad thing. It's actually a good thing.

To the intuitive spirit, failure can be seen as the fastest way to success. From a bigger perspective, some form of failure is actually required to succeed. Hold that thought for now; you don't need to figure it out or totally understand it just yet.

This brings us to the prospecting eagle on the front cover of this book. I was watching a nature show on television years ago and the announcer made the comment that when the eagle dives for a fish, he doesn't catch a fish every time. He can actually miss many times in a row before he catches a fish. Then a thought-provoking question occurred to me.

Does the eagle feel bad because he missed? Does he criticize and berate himself when his timing is off? Does he feel progressively worse each time he misses? Does he think that he needs to change his approach or that he is in the wrong line of work because he missed a few times? No.

Failure, misses, no-shows, busy signals, voicemail, or being stuck in traffic, are all required parts of the process. They have little impact on your overall success if you don't give them any meaning by judging them as positive or negative. And this is one of the key elements of making God's Selection Process work for you. You play the game by dialing the phone and talking to people. What happens after that actually doesn't matter because it's not up to you. With God's Selection Process, God decides what happens.

Of course, you have your part to play. You have to be a catalyst and dial the phone. Then you have to trust your intuitive instincts as you talk to your prospect. When I trust and act on my intuitive instincts, I am being guided by my Higher Self. I feel myself in alignment with God and do what feels intuitively right moment by moment.

In my ongoing research some smart person whose name I can't remember pointed out that *trusting your instincts* is not necessarily the same as *trusting your intuitive instincts*. Your ego's instincts are to survive, avoid discomfort, minimize risk, take as much as you can for yourself, and let other people fend for themselves. Your intuitive instincts are not based on fear of survival and trying to control the results. Your intuitive instincts live in a miraculous world of abundance where everyone gets some version of what they ask for somehow.

Trusting your *intuitive* instincts is crucial. After being a full-time sales performance coach for over thirty years, I am convinced the right brain and its intuition is the smartest and fastest part of the brain.

The left side of the brain and its analytical component is the slowest part of the brain *and* an absolute necessity. We are trained to use the left brain for everything and wonder why we fumble. To the credit of the left brain, it is in charge of vital functions that keep us alive, but it was not meant to make complicated decisions. The left brain is most comfortable with activities that have limited parameters, like adding a column of numbers or proofreading.

If you ask your analytical left brain to help you hit the shot that will win the weekend tournament at the golf club, you're going to be disappointed. The more complicated the challenge, the more the analytical mind is a fish out of water. I have a recent article from the *Harvard Business Review* that basically says you are better off going with your intuitive instincts on complicated issues because the narrow focus of the analytical mind is prone to making obvious mistakes. Your analytical mind doesn't see the big picture and therefore has a poor sense of direction and timing. There is nothing wrong with your left brain, although your critical ego might disagree. We just use it for things it wasn't designed to do, which can end up making us look like one of the Three Stooges.

Another outstanding example of the power of the right brain for making business decisions or complicated decisions of any kind is listening to successful entrepreneurs. The next time you hear an interviewer ask an entrepreneurial genius how they came upon their great success, listen for two main points. Entrepreneurs will say they wished they would have *trusted their intuitive instincts sooner* and, if they had the chance to do it all over again, they would have *made more mistakes faster*. What they are saying is that the keys to their great success are the exact opposite of what you were taught in school with the analytical, academic model.

TIME TO SMILE AND DIAL

Now let's make some prospecting calls.

You have people to call and you are under financial pressure to make some sales. The thought of getting on the phone hooks your ego's desire to keep you safe and risk-free. So now your ego is looking for important things to do besides prospecting.

You maintain your resolve against your ego and get up the nerve to make a few calls and get three instant no's. Your extensive analytical training says that you must be doing something wrong. You have to figure out a better phone approach or make a better offer or find better prospects to call. Something is obviously not working.

Sound familiar? What usually happens next is that your prospecting stops while you try to figure out how to improve your situation. Bottom line: no prospecting means nothing good can happen and the pressure continues to build for another day.

Question: What is the opposite of fear and doubt? *Answer*: Trust and faith.

The most important paradigm shift we can make to increase our prospecting numbers is to trust God's Selection Process instead of negatively judging it as not working. You have heard the saying, "Let go and let God." Or, "Give your problem to God." This means that God is in charge of who you match up with and who you don't, not your controlling ego and its sales techniques. By the way, when you "let go and let God," that doesn't mean there is nothing for you to do. God is counting on you to make a substantial effort in terms of prospecting activity. That's a required part of the deal.

For a person taking the Relationship Builder approach to selling, there are three things required to make a sale: *chemistry, timing,* and *money.*

- *Chemistry* describes an affinity or connection between you and the prospect.

- *Timing* refers to the prospect having a current need for a product or service you have to offer.

- *Money* means the prospect has the resources to buy your product or service.

The most interesting aspect of these three requirements is that they are all *out of your control* during the typical sales cycle, which is commonly a few weeks to a few months. The chemistry is either there or it's not, the timing is either right or it's not, and there is money to buy the product or there's not. Obviously, these conditions can change, but they usually don't change very fast. Chemistry is probably the most important and the least likely to change, which is a good thing. The timing and the money have the potential to adjust in your favor during the sales cycle, but usually require a lot more time to pass for substantial change to occur.

The million-dollar question is, what would it feel like to really let go and let God take over?

First, you stop negatively judging the prospecting process in any way whatsoever. You choose to believe that good things will come your way if you demonstrate a trust and faith in God's Selection Process. You release all negative feelings of tension, anxiety, fear, doubt, worry, etc. Fortunately, you can't do *trust and faith* and *fear and doubt* at the same time.

Let go of the ego's need to control people and do everything correctly. Instead replace your controlling ego with trust and faith in your intuitive ability to think on your feet and respond appropriately in the moment. Remember: with the spirit-based approach, God is in charge, not your ego. Doing things correctly is not the main focus of the spirit; it is *trusting your intuitive instincts*. It's about being real, being your authentic self.

Can you imagine giving up the need to say something perfectly and trusting whatever words come out of your mouth? If you are connected to your Higher Self, what you say is going to work in ways that you may not understand and don't need to understand. What's the worst thing that can happen? You make a call and it doesn't go as you would like it to. No big. You make a mental note on how to deal with that situation for the future if there is anything to notice, and move on to the next call.

Remember: the fastest way to learn is to make more mistakes faster. I don't mean you intentionally try to make mistakes, but you jump in and learn as you go. Your analytical ego will think you've lost your mind, which is accurate to some degree, and it's still the fastest way to learn anything.

Many times in my career I have had a new product to promote. I have found the fastest way to find the best telephone language is to come up with a couple of lines to get the prospecting call started and then *wing it*. This is backwards from our academic training. You are supposed to figure everything out first before you take action. The problem is you will never come up with phone language that will be as good as the language that will come from listening to what you have to say while you are winging it. Your intuition is way smarter than your intellect.

I know this sounds far-fetched, but remember, you are engaging the power and skill of your intuitive spirit which is fearless, has total recall, and has unlimited resources. Your intuitive spirit is an improv genius. You are not accustomed to using this much of your brainpower. You need to experience this for yourself and develop more confidence in your ability to know what to say without thinking or remembering scripted responses.

When you trust your intuitive spirit, you don't have to figure out what to say. You listen to what you are guided to say and then say it. That part of your brain is fast, intelligent, and clever. Would you be willing to know what to say without any preparation and have it work? That is what can happen when you trust your intuitive spirit. But you have to let go to get at it, totally suspend any negative judgment of yourself or of the prospecting process, and keep making calls.

Remember that the key is to make enough calls, not to make a perfect call. *It is only when you prospect enough that you get to see the miracle of business coming to you in both expected and unexpected ways.*

When you make enough calls, you allow the numbers to work in your favor. You are giving God something to work with. When you take action and meet people on the phone or in person, you are creating a way for people to connect with you. When you are interacting with people, you are giving God and yourself the chance to find the right matches.

You have heard the saying, "God helps those who help themselves." Everyone thinks they understand what this means, but it is often misinterpreted by the ego. For our purposes in taking a spirit-based approach to prospecting, it is a statement about the law of required activities. If you risk doing the required activity of prospecting, you will be rewarded.

CONNECTING WITH YOUR HIGHER SELF

Maybe you are saying, "Okay, this all sounds great, but how do you connect with your Higher Self?" This is a crucial element of the spirit-based approach, and requires a combination of knowing what feels intuitively right; being aware of your conscience; and being able to discern who is speaking to you, your controlling ego or your intuitive spirit.

When I am working with a new coaching client who tends to be on the analytical side, I have to get them to use more of their right brain where their intuition lives. Someone pointed out to me that if you are left-handed, the hemispheres are reversed. So for the sake of simplicity and with no disrespect for the lefties, let's assume everyone is right-handed.

The right brain is home to more than just intuition. All the more powerful feelings that we need to get the challenging things done in life are on the right side of the brain. Motivation, inspiration, creativity, ingenuity, our values, our sense of purpose, and possibly our calling are all right-brain neighbors.

The main function of the left side of the brain is to organize and label information for the right brain. It wasn't designed for strategic or creative thinking. Also, the left brain uses energy; it doesn't generate energy like the right brain. When you follow what feels intuitively right, it generates the energy of enthusiasm and you feel good. When you analyze and try to figure things out with linear logic, you need to take breaks to get your energy back.

I used to do a lot of work related to burnout. What I found in my research was that people who are burned-out are not feeling much of anything about their work or, more important, the people they are working with. People who are burned-out are going through the motions with the habits they have established and using their intellect to solve the problems that occur. My conclusion was that if you are not using the part of the brain that generates the energy of enthusiasm, you are going to become a lifeless shell with no heart. That's what it feels like to be burned-out.

Another way to show people the difference between the analytical and intuitive parts of the brain is to liken them to something that is familiar and that we understand. I like to call the analytical mind a *magnifying glass* and the intuition *Google Maps.*

The analytical mind is really good at looking at a tiny space of reality and dealing with the details of that space. For that reason it is not good with the big picture. The analytical mind functions best in a contained environment where the elements it is studying are steady or unchanging. The more complexity and moving parts you add for the analytical mind to deal with, the faster its capacity is diminished to plodding incompetence.

The intuitive side of the brain, on the other hand, loves complexity, and the more moving parts the better. The intuitive brain can process millions of pieces of information per second; the analytical mind is limited to a few. I read an article that said the intellect (analytical mind) could process 2,000 pieces of information per second. That felt extremely high to me and I suspected it was the conclusion of someone who thinks they are being analytical when in fact they are actually being intuitive.

Back to the Google Maps-magnifying glass comparison. Google Maps can zoom out to any distance and zoom in fairly close, but it has limitations once you get close to an object. Then the magnifying glass comes in handy. The analogy is not perfect, but it helps show the difference between the two basic functions. One of the capacities of the intuition is that it can look at the smallest level of detail and make a determination whether things feel right or not. So if you think about it, it's a match made in heaven. One part of the brain has the capacity to deal with an unlimited amount of information all at once; the other side is good with looking at the details, one at a time. In fact, teamwork between both sides of the brain is ideal because if you are all intuition, you have an uncanny sense of timing and direction, but you may have difficulty getting things done. If you are only analytical, you can be good with details and good at the steps required to get things done, but you may be doing the wrong thing at the wrong time and probably working very slowly.

Unfortunately, most of us have not been trained to use the brain with this kind of brilliant teamwork. We have been trained to do everything with the analytical, narrowly focused, left brain, which interestingly becomes a source of fear and doubt. And it makes sense if you think about it. If you are blocking out the part of the brain that can see the big picture, you are going to be headed into a lot of wrong turns and dead ends. It's like looking all over the house for your car keys while you are holding them in your hand. If you expanded your field of vision (or awareness) to include your hand, you would realize you are holding your keys.

For the sake of being dramatic, I like to say that your intellect or your analytical mind is the dumbest, slowest part of the brain, and we have been taught to use it for everything. There is a reason for this. Our academic learning system is based on studying what is observable and provable, step by step. We don't know how to rationalize or justify the fact that the intuition can look at massive amounts of information and come up with the answer to a problem in seconds. The part that scares us the most is that we have no proof that the answer from the intuitive mind will work. We can't see how the intuitive mind came up with its answer. So guess what you have to have in order to trust your intuitive mind? *Trust and faith.*

I think we are actually put here on Earth to learn to have trust and faith in our intuitive instincts, which are what I call the intuitive spirit. I am not saying this is an easy thing to do for there are numerous hazards in our path.

There are a couple of distinctions you have to make for this to work. One is to define what intuition feels like as much as possible, which can be a challenge. I like the phrase, *internal promptings barely caught in the web of human consciousness.* This says that intuitive feelings are incredibly subtle, which makes them harder to feel, hear, or see. Some would describe intuition as *a quiet sense of knowing that something is either right or not right.*

People experience an intuitive feeling in a variety of ways, which complicates the defining process. However, you will find that the folks who are confident about using their intuition have figured out a way to know what is intuition and what is not. I think that is work we all have to do for ourselves. I could go into considerable detail describing what intuition feels like to me, but you may find that you don't relate to much of what I'm saying because it's slightly different for you.

I have found that with a little practice, most people can identify an intuitive hunch, then expand on that awareness. It's also helpful to realize that your intuition can be extremely subtle and easy to miss. Being more patient and aware of the slightest nuance can reveal a direction or a choice. It's very different from the way we've been trained to think and make decisions. It's okay to feel like beginner. I have had coaching clients who started to listen to and trust their intuitive instincts tell me it was the beginning of a whole new life.

Asking yourself "Does the action I'm about to take feel intuitively right?" is a great way to start to become more aware of your intuition. Don't be concerned if you don't get an answer right away. The important thing is to be asking the question. The answers are on their way and they will quietly appear to you at what may seem like odd moments when you are engaged in something totally unrelated.

EMOTION VS. INTUITION

In addition to poor training and mis-education, there are two other big hurdles to knowing what feels intuitively right. One is emotions and the other is your ego.

Emotions are also feelings and are based on something we have experienced in the past. Emotions are usually more intense than intuition and more fickle in that they come and go quickly.

Intuition does not change that fast. If something feels right today, it will feel right tomorrow and next week and for a relatively long period of time. Also, an intuitive answer or an intuitive internal message is not directly related to a past experience as emotions are. I am not saying there is anything wrong with emotions. They are highly useful to get you motivated and have many other purposes, *but they are not intuition.*

The other challenge to recognizing intuition is that the ego has its own form of intuition. What feels right to the ego is different from what feels right to your intuitive spirit. They have different agendas. Your ego is going for survival and acquiring as much for itself as it can. It doesn't particularly care about the welfare of others. Being inclusive is seen as a good thing by the ego (it likes to look good), but it is also a luxury. The ego has to make sure it is taken care of before it can be too generous with its resources.

The intuitive spirit, on the other hand, is unlimited and fearless. It has access to universal intelligence and endless resources. There isn't anything the intuitive spirit can't do with the resources it has. Or, said affirmatively, the intuitive spirit can create anything. It is also caring, loving, kind, generous, solution-oriented, forward-looking, and naturally wants things to work for everyone.

The ego thinks in terms of "you OR me." The intuitive spirit thinks in terms of "you AND me." The intuitive spirit is connected to and part of everything that reflects abundance. The ego sees itself as separated from everything and on its own, thus its focus on survival. This is a vast subject, but as I have stated, my goal is to give you just enough information to get you into action. So let's move on to simple ways to access your intuition.

TWO QUESTIONS

When my coaching clients say, "Okay, I get it. I want to be more intuitive. What do I do?" My response is to give them two questions to start using throughout the day.

The first question is, "What does it feel like it's time to do now?" The second question is, "Who does it feel like it's time to call now?"

Ask yourself these questions at least once an hour to see what happens. When something to do pops into your thoughts unrelated to anything else you are doing, strongly consider doing it. I create a To-Do list every day and prioritize what is most important, but I also listen to my big-picture intuition which can see way more than my near-sighted intellect can.

One day I was busy working in my office and out of nowhere I had the thought to go to Costco. I needed to go to Costco, but it was on my list for later in the week. I said to myself, "Really, go to Costco now? I am working on an important project." The feeling remained strong so I trusted it and headed out for Costco. When I got on the road there was no traffic, so I was there in record time. I had no problem finding what I needed, a miracle in itself. And there was no line when I went to check out. I was there and back in less than a half hour.

So here's the question. Do you think my intuition knew when to go to Costco and get everything done in record time, or was it luck? As you know, any kind of shopping experience can take hours. I got everything done in less than thirty minutes. We have no way to prove that my intuition was the source of my good fortune, which is also one of the great challenges in the way of learning to trust your intuition.

To address this challenge, I took a more academic approach. Why not? That is the way we've all been trained to think. Plus I'm a guy. Guys tend to have a large left brain. So I kept a log of all the times I acted on my intuitive instincts and what happened as a result. The results were quite astounding. It was also interesting to realize that if I had not kept a log, I would have forgotten about most of these experiences. I suspect the ego has something to do with that. Anyway, the results were highly in favor of trusting my intuitive instincts.

I can't say that they were right every time, but certainly my intuition was right way more than it was wrong. Some would go so far as to say that your intuition is always right if you can get really good at knowing what's intuitive and what's not. Most of us don't have the skills to be that good yet. So it's good to acknowledge the downside if your discernment of what's intuitive and what isn't is a little off. If I feel like I can handle the consequences of making a mistake in a specific situation, I've learned to go with my intuitive instincts.

Sometimes it would take awhile to see the brilliance of my intuitive choice. Related to prospecting, I can think of numerous times when it felt intuitively right to give something to someone who was not really interested in being a coaching client. My analytical ego would be asking, "Why are you giving this person a copy of your ebook when they don't seem to be that interested?" My intuitive spirit would be saying, "There is something there; I can't describe it, it's a feeling. I like this person. I feel connected to this person somehow."

Sometimes it took months or even years for that person to come back in my life, but I would see their name again. Maybe they would write a positive book review on Amazon. Some of them referred their friends to me, who became coaching clients. And some of those people who weren't interested called back years later and became clients when their situation had changed. It was more validation for trusting my intuitive instincts: you never know when your kindness or your thoughtfulness is going to come back to you in a big way.

Learning how to discern the different feelings that we all experience is an important skill. There are a variety of feelings that most people are experiencing all the time. As mentioned before, your ego has its own version of what feels right. Your emotions play a powerful role. Your intuitive instincts are often the most important in terms of making choices or choosing a direction and can be the hardest to hear or feel because of the distraction from the other two.

Before we move on, there is one more question to ask yourself that can be helpful in developing your intuitive instincts: *"Does this feel good, or does it feel right."*

Often after I have spoken to an audience and am answering questions, people say that they like that I am telling them to do *what feels good.* They are on the right track, but this is a good spot to make an important distinction. What feels good can also feel right. More often what feels good does not necessarily feel right. For example, if you are committed to losing a few pounds, it will feel good to have another piece of pie, but it probably won't feel right.

It was a vital turning point in my ability to promote my products and services when I finally had the guts to ask myself if it felt right to prospect. The answer from my intuitive spirit was a resounding yes. The answer from my ego was, "This can't be the only way to find clients; there has to be an easier way." Knowing what I now know, I went with my intuitive spirit.

GET QUIET, ASK QUESTIONS, AND LISTEN

Quieting your mind so you can better hear your intuition is imperitive. This can be done in a variety of ways. Some people meditate. Some would call it a daily time of prayer. Exercise, walking, driving, washing dishes, or anything that keeps your conscious mind engaged in doing something simple can facilitate your ability to better hear your intuition. Some of my most profound insights have come to me when I was doing something fairly mindless.

I like a combination of meditation and writing on a yellow legal pad. I do a closed-eye meditation that is a combination of several different approaches. When I become aware of something that feels like an insight, I open my eyes and write down the words. Then I close my eyes again and go back into my meditation.

If you are not into meditation yet, just take some quiet time with a pad of paper or a word processing document. I like to write things down when I process my thoughts and feelings. I also keep ongoing word-processing documents of my insights on a variety of topics. Word-processing documents are much easier to read and store. I have found that the notes on my yellow pad can become a big pile of paper in a short time. So I go through those notes and type the "keepers" into a word-processing document.

The most important aspect of your private session with your Self is to get quiet. Do a ceremony, say a prayer, do something to get you into that quiet zone. *Then ask yourself questions.* Write the questions down on the yellow pad or your laptop and let the answers flow to you. You don't need to figure anything out. This is not a linear thinking process at this point. You are creating a space for intuitive thoughts and feelings to float into your awareness. You are creating a quiet space where you can hear the inner promptings of your intuition without all the distractions of your intellectual ego and your emotions.

This is also a good time to start to identify where your thoughts and feelings are coming from. Do they sound suspiciously like you are playing it safe or do you feel some energy emerging? Does it feel like your thoughts are coming from your past experience or does it feel like something new? Brand new is usually intuitive and often comes with a feeling of elation.

Becoming better able to discern what is intuition, what is emotion, what is coming from your ego, and what is coming from your Higher Self is a lifelong project. The most important thing is that you are working to develop that skill by your practice. Ask yourself questions and listen for the answers and then see if you can sense where the answers are coming from. Your intuitive answers are going to have a certain feel and your ego's answers are going to reflect its controlling agenda.

– *PATTON HYMAN* –

I was introduced to Patton Hyman by one of my longtime coaching clients in the Northeast. Patton has written a wonderful book titled *The Inner Advantage: Applying Mindfulness in Business and Law—and Everywhere Else.* He is a retired partner of a prominent law firm in Atlanta and has been teaching attorneys how to meditate for over twenty years. I recommend his book often to my coaching clients because it is an excellent resource for beginners. Here are a couple of passages from his book related to our discussion:

As we continue meditating, we notice that there are gaps in our thinking, gaps where nothing seems to be happening. As we notice those gaps over and over, we start to appreciate that they're actually not "nothing." These gaps represent glimpses of presence. Although they may seem at first like transitory interruptions in our thinking, as they become more familiar, we realize that the gaps of presence are the norm. Our thinking (at least the habitual, churning thoughts) is the interruption. We can relax with both the gaps and the thoughts and let our natural presence reveal itself more and more.

A parable of presence: *Two young fish are swimming along together in a pond when an old fish approaches from the opposite direction. As the old fish passes he remarks, "How's the water today, fellas?" The youngsters keep on swimming, and then one turns to the other: "What's water?" Presence is like water. And, like the young fish, we may never have noticed the simple experience of presence. Recognizing it begins with acknowledging that we may never have considered whether we're present or not. Until someone flags the issue for us, we may never even think about it.*

– *PARAMAHANSA YOGANANDA* –

Paramahansa Yogananda is my favorite spiritual author and meditation resource. I have read and studied many of his books, which are published worldwide in forty languages. His writing and his teachings are brilliantly clear and understandable. Originally, he was sent to the US from India by his guru in the 1920s with a mission to show the similarities between Hinduism and Christianity. The organization he established in Southern California is called Self-Realization Fellowship, which offers a large collection of practical books, booklets, and audio on how to live life to its fullest (Yogananda-SRF.org).

Yogananda has said many profound things that have greatly affected how I approach life. He talks about having to make many business decisions in his life that involved all kinds of people and resources that represented substantial amounts of money. He says simply that if he trusted his intuition, he never made a mistake in business with people or money. That's an amazing statement and track record.

– *ALBERT EINSTEIN* –

Albert Einstein is also someone I have come to respect through his writing. He is considered to be the most influential physicist of the twentieth century and surely one of the most brilliant minds of modern time. Obviously, I like that he was an advocate of the right brain and its power to create and uncover explanations for the great mysteries of life. Here are some quotes related to our topic:

"Imagination is everything. It is the preview of life's coming attractions."

"The only really valuable thing is intuition."

"We should take care not to make the intellect our god; it has, of course, powerful muscles, but no personality."

"The intuitive mind is a sacred gift. The rational mind is a faithful servant. We have created a society that honors the servant, and has forgotten the gift."

"We shall require a substantially new manner of thinking if mankind is to survive."

"God always takes the simplest way."

"I want to know God's thoughts, the rest are details."

7. SKILL DEVELOPMENT

THE FEEL OF THE CALL

Volumes have been written about how to make sales prospecting calls. I am not going to rehash the conventional wisdom. However, I will tell you how I like to make calls and the skills I think are important as a Relationship Builder.

Simply stated, to be an effective telephone prospector, you need to:

• Be someone people enjoy talking with...

• Be able to establish some credibility and/or expertise...

• Make an intriguing offer to see if your prospect might have an interest...

• Then go wherever the call takes you.

I have spent over three decades both prospecting for my own coaching practice and teaching others how to be more effective at prospecting as a sales performance coach. My goal has always been to find a way to make the prospecting process as enjoyable as possible, even fun. I want to make friends when I call people. I want to see if I can help them in some way, even on a short call. And, of course, I want to make them an offer that is so good it will be hard for them to say no.

My approach to prospecting is the result of many years of trial and correction and is highly refined to fit me and my style and strengths. So the purpose of this chapter is to show you some of the possibilities and then for you to take whatever is useful and disregard the rest. You will want to refine your prospecting process to best fit your style and strengths as I have.

My product is coaching, which is highly intangible. Coaching is a process that is usually defined by the issues the client has and the results the client gets from the engagement. I don't take a structured approach. I trust my intuitive instincts to guide the way. I like to work as fast as possible to get my clients to achieve whatever they are trying to accomplish.

The process is highly customized for each client, depending on their needs and objectives. Certainly, I have *some* structure, but even that structure is loose and adaptable to clients' needs. My goal for my coaching clients is to help them develop their ideal practice. This is accomplished by creating a vision of the ideal and then eliminating any internal conflicts related to their sales process. The goal is to have everything you need to do become as natural as breathing.

Because I have a powerful, unique, somewhat undefined process to introduce to people, I look for a particular kind of potential client: one who is open to cutting-edge approaches, who is willing to try new things, and who will answer the phone and talk for a few minutes when I call.

Who I am being when I call is just as important as the ideal characteristics of my coaching prospects. I want to be outgoing, warm, friendly, compassionate, kind, gentle, understanding, and patient. I want to be determined to make calls and reach my sales activity goals. I expect to do well because I mean well. I attempt to be as inviting and intriguing as possible and at the same time ready to move on to the next person if there is no interest or connection.

Prospecting for me is looking for gold, not trying to turn rocks into gold. The traditional approach to sales teaches you to attempt to convert the rocks, but I have determined that's more work than it's worth. It's much easier to limit your practice to looking for gems and tossing the rocks. It's also a lot more fun.

My calls have a social feel. I perceive them as more of a public relations call than a sales call. If someone shows interest in me and my work, I try to help them on the initial call as much as possible and give them access to some of my materials as a way for them to get to know me. I approach my prospecting with the vision of making friends. My relationships with my coaching clients all close. In many cases, I know them better than anyone else in their life, especially if I have worked with them for many years. So I see my prospecting process as looking for future clients/friends, which is a more rewarding and meaningful approach for me.

I am looking for people who want to grow and want help. I like to tell people that they don't need a coach. You will figure out how to reach the level of success you are after on your own, eventually. The reason you hire a coach is to cut years off the learning curve. I am looking for people who want to speed up the process and enjoy working with someone as a team. I have hired many coaches in my career for a variety of purposes and find I accomplish much more having another pair of objective eyes looking at what I am doing. I also like the energy and synergy that come from conversing with a silent partner who is totally dedicated to helping me find the best path to greater success.

MY LANGUAGE

Usually, I can tell how open people are by how they answer
the phone. The first thing I say to people is, "Hi, _____, this
is Sid Walker. How are you?" I say that with as much warmth,
friendliness, and sincerity as I can generate. I want people to
feel my presence and my confidence as a person, not as a
salesman.

If the person responds in a pleasant, respectful way with
"Great. Sid. How are you?" I have a live one. If they respond
with "What are you selling?" "How did you get my number?"
"I am really busy. What is it that you want?" or a grumpy
hello or some other negative response, I may just hang up or
say I dialed the wrong number. I have no interest in talking to
negative-sounding people. It is a waste of time for my
practice. I have no interest in coaching people in sales who
treat other people with such blatant disrespect. I know that
sounds judgmental, but it's how I qualify my potential clients.
I have had enough experience to know that grumpy, frustrated
people are not going to hire me.

There is a moment of truth at the beginning of the call when I
can feel how I am being judged by the prospect. If the feeling
is negative, I will wind up the call quickly. If the feeling is
neutral or positive, I will keep going. Sometimes I can feel a
slight negative judgment, but there is also a willingness to hear
what I have to say. I have learned to give those people a
chance because they often warm up if we keep talking.

Assuming I have a positive response with their hello, the next
thing I want to do is tell them I will just keep them a second,
tell them what I do, establish my credibility, and involve them
in the conversation somehow.

I will say something like, "John, I will just keep you a second.
I have been a coach for thirty years and XYZ Company is one
of my biggest clients. I have helped a lot of people become
leaders in your company and I'm sure we know a lot of the

same people. Also, I see you're on the list of people making some money, so congratulations." Then I wait for a response.

At this point, I usually get a thank-you or a laugh and a friendly joke like "What list is that?"

Then I proceed with, "John, I have one quick question for you. I have a proven knack for helping people develop their ideal practice. I have more psychological depth than most coaches and I'm really good at helping people build on their strengths. I was wondering if that sort of thing is of any potential interest to you?"

My language has added more definition and credibility about what I do and then ended with an inviting and intriguing offer. I am being as open and genuine as possible at this point. I don't want them to feel any sales pressure or that I am leading them in any way. I want them to feel that I am an honorable guy with a legitimate offer and want their honest response, whatever it is.

Sometimes people say, "Not really," and then proceed to give me a short explanation, which is fine. I wish them well and get off the phone. If there is no interest, I don't offer them something in the hopes that they might become interested someday. I have found that to be a waste of time. However, if I like the person, I may offer them something that I suspect might be of interest if it feels right. Sometimes is just feels good to give.

Most often, I get the respect of a positive response. People say they are working with a coach, or they have worked with a coach, or they have been thinking about hiring a coach, or that several of their friends seem to like having a relationship with a coach. Then the conversation goes on from there. At this juncture, if we are talking about coaching, I have a potential new candidate for coaching or webinars or my products. The main thing is that I have identified someone who is interested in coaching and so far likes what I have to say to the degree that they are still talking and will likely want to get more information about what I do.

THE CONNECTION

I'm a keyboard musician. I like to envision my calls as a form of jazz or improv. I am comfortable with this style. There is some structure to my call, but it is also very loose. I like to be able to go in any positive direction the prospect wants to go and have some fun with the call. I want to demonstrate right away that my style is totally about them and helping them see their strengths and develop those strengths. It's always meaningful when someone comments that they like my style on the phone.

I call financial advisors, who you can bet are paying close attention to how I am handling the call I am making to them. Who I am being and how I approach the call are a demonstration of my coaching skills and an advertisement for my coaching service. That's one of the reasons I like to do telephone prospecting. It's an effective way to take an intangible product like coaching and make it more real for the person I am calling.

Looking for a connection with my prospect is also important to me. A connection is a feeling that can be difficult to describe, but you know it when you have it. It is usually based on level of rapport or chemistry. Sometimes it is similar background. It can be similar values and style. I am an expert on the low-key approach to selling, which is of great interest to many people who are tired of the pushy and controlling traditional approach. I am looking for kindred spirits. These are people who want to grow and develop based on their style and strengths. Since this is my passion, if someone else has a similar interest, there is going to be connection. If there is a connection, there is a good chance we are going to do business at some point.

Another quality I am looking for in a prospect is that they move toward me or come partway. Even though I was taught like everyone else to try to talk people into things, I have learned that is not the best approach as a Relationship Builder. If I want the sale more than my prospect does, it's going to mean extra work that I don't want. I am going to have to keep reselling them every time they run into doubt, resistance, or skepticism about what they bought.

I come right out and tell people, "I don't want to work with you unless it feels right to you." Otherwise, it takes too much of my energy. I like to work with motivated clients who want to learn and are willing try new things. I don't want to be attempting to drag resistant, skeptical people into the light.

Trusting the no's is another way to make this point. If you have a heart-to-heart talk with a potential client and the conclusion is not to proceed, don't keep trying to talk them into a sale.

I teach financial advisors that their main job today as a Relationship Builder is to help their clients make an informed decision that feels right to them (the client). It is not about trying to talk people into buying a product. I call that old school and less evolved. I find it much more empowering and fun to help the client make an informed decision that feels right than to try to control or lead them into a corner where I'm pushing them to buy my product. If you want a real relationship with the prospect or client, you have to honor what feels intuitively right to them. Anything short of that truth feels like smoke and mirrors.

A fascinating thing sometimes happens when I present the idea of putting your client's interests first and helping them make informed decisions that feel right to them.

I did a three-hour live seminar for a large life insurance agency years ago. At the conclusion of the seminar, a young guy came up to me and said, "I really like that you put your client's interests ahead of your own and you help people get what they really want. And I am going to take that approach as soon as I'm successful." Unbelievable. He missed the whole point.

People new to sales are often so brainwashed to push for sales that they consider helping people get what they want a luxury for later when they don't need to make sales. Helping people make informed decisions that feel right to them is actually your *guarantee* of success as a Relationship Builder and will double your sales or better.

You are going to get objections when you prospect. You will want to collect your best answers to common objections and see if that allows you to continue the conversation. A common objection for financial advisors is, "I already have an advisor." The way we usually handle that objection is to say something like, "John, I understand. It is rare I that I meet people who don't have one or more advisors. But that wouldn't mean we couldn't get together, because here's what I'll do. Let me share my ideas on how to maximize what you're doing with your money and then if you like the ideas, you can take them to your advisor. Fair enough?"

For as a relationship builder this is a powerful response for a couple of reasons. First, if the prospect agrees to this, there is room for you. He is not totally in love with his advisor. Second, if you are better at connecting with the client than the other advisor is, you will likely end up with the business. Most people want a real relationship with their trusted advisors. Most salespeople have not been taught to connect with the client, which means you can earn the business away from the competition fairly easily if you develop a stronger relationship with the client.

When I work with my coaching clients on telephone skills, one of my main premises is to be hard to say no to. Offer so much that it would be crazy for them to say no. Here is an example with a referral opening:

"Hi, John. This is Sid Walker. How are you? [John responds.] Good. I will just keep you a second.

"I was referred to you by Jerry Smith. You know Jerry, right? [John responds.] Okay, great.

"Jerry had some very complimentary things to say about you. He said you are a _____. [Let John respond.]

"What I do, John, is help people maximize what they are doing with their conservative money.

"What I typically like to do is spend an hour together. I will give you as much information as I can on whatever topics are of greatest interest to you. I will answer as many questions as I can. I don't charge for this meeting and there's nothing to buy at this point.

"I can typically make or save people thousands of dollars, even tens of thousands of dollars, from this single meeting!

"Does that sound like that might be worth you and I spending some time together?"

You need to be ready for a knee-jerk cautious response. It is normal for people not to jump and say yes even if they like your offer. Be ready with more language that backs up your first pitch.

"I like this way of doing business, because I find most everyone else does. This gives you and me a chance to meet. You get to see me in action. I will more than pay for the time we spend together.

"My main goal is to give you as much useful information as possible in our time together. I have no thought you are in the market to buy anything at this point. This gives us a chance to get to know each other and for me to establish myself as a resource to you for the future. That sounds like a fair approach, doesn't it, John?"

THE INDEX CARD

When I prospect, I write down the names of the people I call on a lined, 6 x 10 index card. I circle the ones I talk to and make notes where appropriate. If you do three columns of names, there is room for fifty names on the lined side of the card. I find fifty dials to be a good phoning session unless I have five promising conversations, which trumps the fifty dials. Once I get my five conversations with prospects showing some interest, that's a good day for me.

At the very top of the card, I usually write one sentence I have found to be the most important single thought for my session. "My job is to dial the phone with the right attitude; the rest is up to God." This gives me a great sense of freedom and hope. All I have to do is dial the phone and let the powers that be determine everything else. This makes prospecting infinitely easier. I also include letting God (my intuitive instincts) decide what I am going to say to each person after my opening lines. It turns out that God is pretty good on the phone!

I have standard lines to open a conversation, but then I have trust and faith in whatever happens instead of being obsessed about doing anything in a predetermined way. To worry about what I'm going to say after the first few lines is way too intellectual, which distracts me from being my intuitive best. Worrying about how I am doing drives me into judging and evaluating what is happening. This invites my limited-thinking ego back into the game, which I want to avoid in every possible way.

My more intuitive approach could be called "winging it" and is a far cry from the controlling and leading techniques we have all been taught to use. What I have found as a Relationship Builder is that the more you try to control the conversation, the less of a relationship you develop. A connected relationship is based on mutual trust and respect with totally open communication. If you try to control people, they feel it and either pull away or go on the defensive. I don't want a relationship with someone trying to control me. Why would I think my prospect, my potential new client and friend, would want any less?

I like to think that most of the elements of my prospecting call are out of my control. I also like to think that if I treat people with honor and respect, God will help both me and the prospect make the right decision.

The parts you *do* control on a call are:

• *Your intent...*

• *Your attitude...*

• *Your language and how you deliver it.*

If you call to connect with people and then make an interesting and intriguing offer with your heart in the right place, you are going to have some good conversations that will turn into sales.

8. CREATING A MENTAL WARM-UP

THE WARM-UP

One of the best ways to prepare yourself for action is a *warm-up*. It's like stretching before you do anything physical. You want to get your muscles ready before you get into action so you are less likely to get injured. The same principle applies to prospecting. You want to get your head thinking the right thoughts and the rest of you feeling good so you are at your best when someone answers the phone.

A warm-up for me is usually something written and represents the most empowering perspective for what I have to do.

It could be a bigger perspective or a new paradigm that creates a thought or feeling that opens the way for me to be able to take action. This focus culminates in a feeling of power and ability that I can use to propel myself into action. I can also re-create and repeat this experience as needed.

There is no limit to how good you can get at anything if you can get a feel for what you are trying to do. An important part of that feeling comes from the mental warm-up to get you into the bigger perspective. When it comes to prospecting or anything you are resisting, the mental warm-up can be a mighty force.

I have collected hundreds of warm-up ideas and discover new ones all the time. I will share the most effective warm-up ideas I know for prospecting. You will discover your own unique thoughts and feelings when you risk taking action.

If you come up with a good warm-up idea, I'd love to hear about it. Send me an email with your breakthrough idea or phrase.

The purpose of the warm-up in the context of prospecting is to create a window that allows you to take action despite any resistance you may be feeling. Being able to take action is crucial and usually requires some extra motivation. You want to keep looking for anything that helps you get into action.

The last part of this chapter is *The Warm-Up Library*. This is a collection of short concepts, ideas, philosophies, phrases, and other one-liners designed to override your ego's resistance and inspire you into action. Some of the ideas I present are similar, but there are subtle changes in the words or language used to describe the idea. Sometimes changing one word can create a breakthrough. I have also included some one-liners as a review of the big-picture solutions presented in Chapter 5.

Your first assignment is to find ideas that launch you into action. You should feel like you are on a treasure hunt for the words, thoughts, language, pictures, etc., that will drive you to take the action you want to take.

Start a word processing document of your favorite phrases. If you are reading a Kindle or digital version of this book, it is easy to highlight and then go back and copy and paste your favorites into a document later. If you are reading the softcover version of the book and you don't want to type your warm-up, investigate a Speech to Text app. You may already have this ability on your cell phone or computer. I have a coaching client who keeps her warm-up in the Notes app of her iPhone that she dictated to Siri.

Read your warm-up every time before you prospect or prepare to take action.

You will also find that you need to change your phrases from time to time. What works today may not be as effective next week. Sometimes I have to change my warm-up daily. That's normal: your ego is diabolically creative at dulling the edge of your breakthroughs.

– WHAT TO EXPECT –

As you repeatedly read your warm-up, these thoughts and feelings will become part of you. You will find yourself replacing the old thoughts created by your protective ego with new empowering thoughts that push you into action. You will notice that certain warm-up phrases will consistently work. You are on a search for the phrases that have the most horsepower.

The good news is that as you experience feelings that open the way for you to take action, you will be able to remember those feelings and use them to overpower your ego's resistance now and in the future. You will get to the point where you can simply feel the resource state of your warm-up and start dialing. You are still warming up, but you are doing it in just a few seconds.

It's okay if your window or opening doesn't happen overnight. You can have an instant breakthrough that can work for a session and then lose it. You can get the breakthrough back. It may take some trust and faith, some repetition, and some creativity.

Small increments of success are a big deal. Don't discount baby steps, because they add up if you keep making them. Your ego tends to be grandiose and wants to solve all problems in one grand movement, which almost never works.

That's part of the ego's genius; it will come up with brilliant ideas that don't cause anything to change.

So if you can feel a glimmer of light or hope, that's huge. I have had these little breakthroughs many times in my life. As I looked for ways to shift my thinking to a bigger perspective, I would get an insight that would give me a rush of energy. Sometimes I would use the inspiration to make a few prospecting calls and experience someone saying yes to my offer. It all seemed so easy for a few moments...I would wonder why I had been avoiding making calls for so long. Then my resistance would come back as I imagined making more calls.

The important thing was that I experienced a tiny breakthrough that allowed me to make some calls and experience some success. That experience made me think I could probably find another new perspective that would help me make more calls. Build on any success you have, no matter how small it may be.

Another thing to remember: no matter how negative you are feeling about yourself and what you have to do, *you can push yourself into action.*

I have experienced some of the worst anxiety attacks in my life just before I picked up the phone for a prospecting session. You can nudge yourself into action by taking the first step, like dialing the phone. Then the intensity of the anxiety will dissipate fairly quickly. If you are making prospecting calls, as soon as someone answers on the other end, your ego has a whole new set of problems to deal with, which diffuses the anxiety. So don't let the intensity of your negative feelings scare you away if you feel like you are about to pass out or throwup. It's all part of the ego's conspiracy to keep you from taking any risks.

I'm sure you have seen footage of professional athletes getting sick before they go into a big game. In Steven Pressfield's insightful book on overcoming the resistance to being creative,

The War of Art, he says, *"Henry Fonda was still throwing up before each stage performance, even when he was seventy-five. In other words, fear doesn't go away. The warrior and the artist live by the same code of necessity, which dictates that the battle must be fought anew every day."*

I once saw an opera diva being interviewed on *60 Minutes.* She was a beautiful woman with captivating charm and an amazing voice. She made $40,000 per performance, and that was about 1995. The interviewer asked her if she had any stage fright. She replied that she was an emotional disaster before each performance standing there waiting for the curtain to open. She would wonder if she could do it again. She would wonder why she didn't choose to be a housewife and avoid all this pressure and madness. But she said the most amazing thing happens when the curtain opens and she can feel the audience and hear their applause. She said she was taken into another world where she became a channel for the music, which was all-consuming, and stayed there for the duration of the performance.

It's normal for athletes, actors, and singers to be an emotional wreck before they perform, and we are no different. When you do things that are challenging, that require all your skill, awareness, and ability to think on your feet, that's pressure. Of course, your ego is horrified that you would put yourself through such torture. Ironically, it is actually your ego that is creating all the fear and doubt.

One of my speaking coaches (I've hired many) used to say to me that *butterflies* are good; it means everything is turned on and ready to perform.

So getting into action doesn't mean that you have no fears, doubts, worries, or anxiety. The ego is here to stay and it's the source of all the negative thoughts and feelings. But you can learn to recognize the ego and its tricks and push the negative angst to one side and turn the volume down to almost zero. The more you practice detaching from your ego's resistance, the better you get at it. And accept the fact that it can be a battle because your ego is on a mission and it's as smart as you are.

The good news is that you have more power than your ego. You can choose to take the stage regardless of what your ego is telling you. Who you really are has the power to ignore the ego's suspicious advice. Your ego also does not want you to know that you have that kind of power and will try to distract you and make you forget.

– THE PAYOFF –

Is it worth doing the things that scare you, the things that you know in your heart you need to do?

Is it worth the effort to put yourself through this emotional and mental trauma?

Not everyone will answer yes to those questions, but those who have taken the risk before will say, "Absolutely." When you risk doing something you are afraid to do or don't think you can do, those are life-changing moments. I can think of numerous things I have done that have scared me silly at different times in my life. Summoning the nerve to ask a pretty woman out on a date either in person or by telephone. Making a telephone call to get a job interview. Taking a ski jump that put me twenty feet in the air at high speed. Playing music and singing in front of an audience. Public speaking in front of hundreds of people. And finally, the one I do battle with on a regular basis, prospecting for coaching clients and all the other forms of self-promotion.

Make a list of the times you have chosen to do something risky or were scared to proceed. You have probably forgotten many of them. And it doesn't have to be a list of the world's greatest accomplishments. If something scared you and you did it anyway, it counts as a breakthrough experience. Let me further qualify that the kind of risk I'm talking about is something that felt right, not an act of recklessness or carelessness. I'm talking about the times when you knew what you needed to do and you did it no matter how scared you were. See if those weren't some of the turning points of your life in terms of your self-confidence and self-esteem.

Sometimes when I'm having trouble making decisions or I'm feeling like a total chicken, I remind myself of the times I took the risk and did the thing I wanted to do. Those are moments of truth. Those are moments that will always be just a thought away, ready to relive again and again as you need them.

There is a lyric in a song from the musical *Hello Dolly* that perfectly reflects the power of a moment of truth: *It only takes a moment to be loved a whole life through...*

In the same way, one breakthrough moment when you risked taking action can give you a lifetime of confidence to do it again and again, especially if you keep choosing to take action. Your confidence will build.

THE WARM-UP LIBRARY

The first section of the Warm-Up Library is *The Ego Barrier*, which is an abbreviated recap of the challenge against taking action presented by your overly cautious, scared, controlling ego. The remaining sections—*Action / Time, Reality, Resource States, Mental Tricks / One-Liners*, and *Spirit-Based*—are a collection of short descriptions of paradigm shifts to a bigger perspective.

Find your favorites and have them ready to go! Your ego is always watching and can't wait to give you its advice. Being able to counter the negative chatter of your ego is your best chance for finding the nerve to dial the phone or do whatever you need to do.

– THE EGO BARRIER –

• The ego creates a wall of flames to make you fearful. The flames are an illusion. If you stick your finger in the flames (dial the phone), the flames instantly disappear, just like in the movies.

• It makes sense to make the calls from a bigger perspective. It is your scared, misguided, childish ego that doesn't want to risk what is required to have the success you are capable of achieving.

• The fear (false ego-evidence appearing real) feels real, but it isn't based on anything that is happening now. However, the money that comes from making calls is very real.

• This is a test of your courage. You need to rise to the occasion. You have to get psyched up to override the ego's natural resistance to taking any kind of risk. Tell Scared Guy and Anal Guy to take a break and give the reins to Outgoing Guy and Resourceful Guy who can make something good happen.

• Your ego is as smart as you are and it's usually trying a lot harder to keep you off the phone than you are trying to get on it. You have to draw on all your strength and intelligence to overcome your ego's bag of tricks.

• Ignore the ego chatter. Your ego's information is flawed because it is based on other people's opinions of you and the illusion of being separated from Source. The ego is a scared little kid who is afraid he may not survive.

• Put all the ego's baggage on the departing train and find the space (opening, window, resource state) with no fear, doubt, worry, or anxiety. Then make calls from that space.

• Resistance is normal. It is built into the way the mind works. Diffuse or weaken the fear, and the resistance goes away or at least is easier to push through. Less fear means less resistance.

- If you are agonizing over who to call and when to call them, your are in your ego-monkey brain. Of course, you can make general qualifications on who and when to call. Generally speaking, the best approach is to *call 'em all, starting right now!*

- Another indicator that you are thinking too much is that you're listening to your ego make up its Disney fantasy about who it thinks people are and whether they need your product. Most often, the truth is that you have no idea about anyone's real situation until you talk to them. *Thank your ego for sharing and dial!*

- Your ego is your source of doubt. Your ego will be the first to let you know if something is not working and will point out that *you* must be doing something wrong.

- The goal of the ego is to deal with the immediate threat, which is to get you out of perceived danger. Dealing with the real issue is never a priority—that can wait until later.

- The right question is, "Does it feel intuitively right to make these calls?" Not "Do I *want* to make these calls?" Your ego knows it *should* prospect, but if it senses any risk or danger, it has to resist.

- All of your fear comes from your ego trying to protect you by reminding you of the negative things that have happened in the past, which can make you feel scared, doubtful, and full of anxiety.

- If you feel fear or resistance, you are giving your ego the stage. If you find any negative thoughts sneaking back into your awareness, you have let the ego stick his nose in your tent.

- The ego is relentless. It constantly judges and evaluates. It never stops. It is never going away.

– ACTION / TIME –

• Taking action is the most important step. Nothing can happen in your favor until you dial the phone. You start the process of creating a new relationship with someone when you push those buttons.

• You engage more of your brainpower in action. You are smarter. In action, you have an increased ability to think on your feet.

• Just do it. It *is* that simple, but that doesn't mean it's easy. This reality favors the doer more than the thinker. If you can take action while trusting your intuitive instincts, you are at your best.

• Push yourself to dial. If there is no possibility of failure, there is no possibility of success.

• Putting in the time is more important than anything else. Do the work, do your service.

• All you have to do is put in the time with the right attitude. Don't judge what happens as good or bad. Just do it.

• Spend more time making calls and go for bigger numbers; you will have breakthroughs.

• What is more important than doing the required activities toward your vision? Nothing. Do the required activities intuitively, and you will be at your best.

• What are the required activities toward the visions that feel right? That is the work of the day.

• Stop being a wimp about doing the required activities. Be aggressive with your resolve, but easy on other people.

• Be outRAgeous: do the *Required Activities* toward your vision/goal.

- To think that you can get away without making calls is opening the door to struggle and stress far greater than that of actually making the calls.

- Action tends to diffuse fear. When you take action, your ego shifts from being afraid to make the call to focusing its attention on dealing with the call you are making.

- Push yourself to make the call. You don't have to push the person you are calling. Let them do whatever they do. And, you can push people if that's your style.

– *REALITY* –

- Prospecting is a part of life that everyone has to do. We have to make choices about all kinds of things. Prospecting is asking people to decide whether the valuable service you are offering might be of interest.

- If other people are having success with their prospecting, that is your proof that it works. It can be helpful to have the statistics of other people who have made calls so you can see this is a worthwhile activity. You are not "going where no one has gone before." However, you might feel like you are the only one agonizing over making calls. Everyone has to deal with this issue because we all have a protective ego that doesn't want us to prospect.

- Whoever you are calling are people just like you. Yes, we all have different backgrounds, training, and experiences. We all have a separate reality and have a different point of view because we occupy our own space that no one else can share. But our basic needs are still the same. We all have dreams, desires, challenges, wants, needs, etc. If you have a worthwhile product, someone is going to be interested.

- The numbers work if you let them. You are guaranteed success either from the calls you make or from the mystical momentum that is created by the commitment of your action.

- Stop thinking you can fail at prospecting. Your success is guaranteed. If you make the calls with the right attitude (the right expectations) and a decent offer, good things are going to happen. There will be winners and losers, which you can handle if you remember that it doesn't matter what happens on any one call.

- You have to like being a catalyst, a leader of sorts. You need to like being a stimulus, a spark, a prod, a nudge. You have to start the process of finding the right match.

- You have to be an initiator, a beacon of light that gives people an option to have a better, easier way. This is such an important quality that it is a major factor in determining whether people will be successful or not.

- If you are on the phone talking to people and making an offer, you are making money.

- The results are what they are; they don't mean anything. Make your calls and don't look back. Improve where you can, but don't waste time judging and evaluating how your session went. Just feel good that you made the calls. You did your job.

- The more you make calls with the right frame of mind, the more you will see you can do it. Your confidence will grow. You will always have to defuse your ego's resistance.

- There is the moment of truth when I can feel whether people are going to judge me negatively when I call. It happens when I say, "Hi, _____, this is Sid Walker. How are you?" I can tell you how the call is going to go based on how the person responds to my opening hello. But that is all out of my control. So I just notice if a judgment is there or not and keep going. If it's a small judgment, the minor discomfort only lasts for a second. If it's a major negative judgment, I get off the phone and don't give it another thought. To be okay with letting people judge you is a powerful ability.

- People not being interested in my offer is totally okay and is not a reflection of the value of me or my product. Your product is not for everyone, even if your well-meaning sales manager tells you it is.

- When you get someone who is not interested, pretend you are fishing and you just caught a fish too small to keep. Toss 'em back in the water!

- When you want to quit prospecting, ask yourself, "What else is there to do right now that is *more* important?"

- Yes, there are easier ways to make a living, but you would likely be bored, frustrated, and unfulfilled by them if it feels right to be prospecting. If it doesn't feel intuitively right to be prospecting, you should find a different job.

- If you make your calls, you will drive business in the door. Even if your calls are not producing much, business will find its way to you.

- Prospecting is a required activity if you need clients. If you think you can skip this step because you're smarter than other people, you'll have to learn the hard way—that is not a smart move.

- You have been given a great opportunity. There is some effort required on your part. Give it your best effort!

- If you feel that horrible feeling that this will never work, all hope is lost, or some other version of total despair, thank your ego for sharing and keep dialing. Your mood will change when something good happens. Nothing good can happen unless you keep dialing.

- Everyone who prospects faces the same challenge. That's why a lot of people can't do sales. They can't hold the vision that a successful call is coming their way while they are seemingly failing on calls that go nowhere.

- How people respond doesn't matter. You get paid for dialing and talking! If the conversation isn't progressing, get off the phone and make the next call.

- When I watch people doing manual labor in the hot sun from my office window, I remind myself that there is no heavy lifting with prospecting and my office is air-conditioned.

- Prospecting requires a mental toughness and discipline to ignore the negative judgments from your own mind as well as the negative judgments of others.

- It's a waste of time to judge the prospecting process because it is almost all out of your control. The only thing you really have any control over is dialing the phone, what you say, and your attitude. Your ego thinks you control everything; your intuitive spirit knows different.

- Negative thoughts weaken the power of your creative capacity.

- If you have a lot of negative thoughts about something you need to do, it may be that you are being tested where you are weak and shown where you need to be strong.

- You can do anything until you judge it negatively. Then you won't want to continue.

- To change your results, you have to change how you think and how you react to things you have seen before.

- Life is different than I expected. What works in life is different from what I was taught to believe by the well-meaning but misinformed egos of other people.

- It's okay to let people judge you, and you don't need to be a doormat. If people are negative toward you, excuse yourself from the conversation. You don't need to continue to honor their negativity.

- You will have calls with negative, angry, frustrated people. There are a lot of them out there. They are not evil people, but they have let their negativity take over.

- People with bad attitudes are a waste of time. Not because they are bad people, but because they are too much work to turn around if you are a Relationship Builder.

- How would you feel about phoning if you really knew you were making money with each dial—lots of money? Prospecting is a form of delayed gratification—an important lesson.

- You have to do the work. There is no success with no effort. You can be lucky, but luck can't sustain success.

- Do you want to feel a sense of accomplishment with a potential payoff? Or do you want to coast and deal with reality tomorrow? A little coasting is okay, just don't make it a habit if you need to prospect.

– RESOURCE STATES –

- Get the right guys or gals driving your prospecting bus. You need Outgoing Guy, Catalyst Guy, Fearless Guy, Resourceful Guy, Intuitive Guy, and Caring Guy. Add anyone else you think would be helpful to you.

- Outgoing Guy and Resourceful Guy will do the heavy driving. Get Anal Guy and Scared Guy away from the driver's seat. Prospecting isn't their thing. Then get Resourceful Guy to make an intriguing offer. If the other person isn't interested, that's the end of it. Make the next call. That's all there is to it!

- The quality of who you are being and the value of what you are offering will affect the response of the other person.

- The people who have the least resistance to prospecting are the least affected by how other people respond to their offer. If you separate the value of what you do from whether someone is interested in your product, it doesn't matter how they respond. Sure, you would like them to be interested, but if they're not interested, it doesn't take away from the value of what you do. You intuitively know someone will be interested in your offer and your expertise, if you believe in its value.

- You have to believe that prospecting will work on some level or it's going to be hard to acquire the energy you need to dial the phone.

- Don't think. Dial. If you think about prospecting, you're going to negatively judge and evaluate what is happening and then want to find something else to do besides prospect.

- Don't think about what you are doing; just do it. Before you know it, you're done for the day. You have done the hard part. You have been a good provider. You went hunting and shot dinner for the family.

- If you judge, you lose. If you doubt, you lose. If you judge or doubt, you lose to your scared, chicken ego.

- Go for feeling good because you reached your sales activity goal for the day, then go do whatever you want!

- Find joy in the completion of doing what needs to be done for today. If you worry about tomorrow, you're allowing negativity to take away from today's success.

- You are fishing to find your clients. You are fishing for the right match.

- You are looking for gold. It's a waste of time to try to turn rocks into gold if you are a Relationship Builder.

- It helps to imagine your best clients, the people who love you. Think of them and the great relationship you have.

Then remind yourself you are looking for more people just like them and that they are out there waiting for you to call.

• Work the phone in a relaxed, steady manner. Enjoy making calls and trust the process. Be at peace with it. You don't need to push people or fight with their negativity to survive.

• When you talk with people, you are looking for an opening of some kind. This is a pointer to your potential clients.

• Treat people with loving kindness, or end the call. Don't let other people's negativity suck you into being negative.

• Practice detachment, patience, and compassion for how people respond to you rather than letting your ego judge and fight back with an irritated tone.

• Do your phoning without fanfare. The most important thing is to do it and give it all the skill you can summon. Then don't judge the results.

• Sometimes I have to bring my energy up to a whole new level before I can get on the phone. It's like I have to be twice as awake. I need to feel some excitement. Start with some stretches, then do some jumping jacks, or run in place and then finish with a loud cowboy "Yee-haw!"

• It's your turn to bat again. It doesn't matter how many times you have struck out in a row; swing for the fence. Or you could go for a base hit, but you want the pitcher to think you're going for the fence. Either way, it's better to be accused of looking at the world through rose-colored glasses than to be called a skeptic.

• Envision and expect that the good call is on its way. You need to dial some duds to get to the good ones. Relax and enjoy yourself. It's all working in your favor.

• Envision the possibility that the next call could be a new client.

- Look forward to the good call, anticipate in your favor, imagine the great call will be the next call. Forget about the calls that didn't work.

- One of my mentors said there are only two reasons to ever look back. One is to see how far you have come, and the other is if someone owes you money.

- Create and hold the vision that you make money with every call regardless of what happens.

- To risk, to engage, to walk out on the stage to give your talk, to push yourself out of the starting gate, to take the face-off in hockey, to take the pitch in baseball, to dial the phone in prospecting: you have to do the thing that starts the process that will allow you to eventually succeed. If you don't start the process, you can't succeed.

- It's a mistake to think about what will happen or what could happen—this is a giant distraction. You actually don't know what will happen, and to think about it takes your mind away from the focus that allows you to be at your best.

- You have to find the window of trust and faith with no negatives and keep that window open. Otherwise your ego will judge and evaluate what it thinks is happening. If you negatively judge prospecting as not working, why would you continue to do it? Your ego wins, you lose.

- What would it feel like to give up all negative thoughts?

- How do you react to pressure, setbacks, blocks, challenges, and delays? Do you see these events as negative, or can you see them as just part of the process of succeeding?

- The Cone Zone of no negative judgment is a room in your mind where you are protected from negative thoughts and judgments. This is also what it feels like to be an intuitive spirit.

- The Cone Ceremony: play dramatic organ music while you imagine lowering the cone of unseen power and protection from negative thoughts over your being.

- Suspend all negative thoughts, feelings, and visions. Then make calls and see what happens.

- If you could feel just as successful with a call that went nowhere as a call that worked, you would be happier and able to make more calls. Not allowing what happened on the last call to keep you from making the next call is a required skill.

- Instead of burning up your energy worrying about how to make perfect calls, make calls and wing it while practicing not caring about what happens on any one call.

- You have a choice between a positive, negative, or neutral vision. A positive vision is the most powerful and adds to your life. A neutral vision is more powerful than a negative vision. A negative vision takes away. The creative part of your brain doesn't know the difference; it just creates. You are better off eliminating the negative visions.

- As a Relationship Builder fishing for potential clients, you are looking for people who are open and interested in improving their lives.

- Phoning is a form of improv. Create a positive expectation. Be in the moment, trust your instincts, trust what comes to you, and put it out there with some flair.

- Feel a desire to help people who want help. Find a passion to make the world a better place through the people you touch every day.

- Develop the guts, the power, and the skill to make prospecting calls and also have intuition and loving-kindness play a key role.

– *MENTAL TRICKS / ONE-LINERS* –

• When you want to quit, make ten more dials. Something good will happen if you keep making calls. If you don't have any more success in that prospecting session, you will at least feel like you put in the effort, which is what counts more than anything else.

• Making prospecting calls is a kind of performance. It's like speaking or singing in front of an audience, or playing in a tournament; there is pressure to perform. This pressure is not something to be afraid of. Use it to inspire yourself to be at your best. It will make this work much more interesting and rewarding. Actually, fear and excitement are similar feelings. Shift your perception from a fear of making the call to an excitement about making the call.

• Don't let the negativity of others touch you. Protect yourself; don't buy into it. Fight it off, move away from it. Don't try to enroll negative people. It's too much work.

• It's best to be in the present moment when you prospect or do any kind of required activity. If you move out of the present moment, you shift into the past-based consciousness of the ego with all its negative judgments and fears. Strong resistance to doing what you need to do is close behind.

• Don't let people's lack of interest take away from your enthusiasm. You can't let other people's negativity affect your attitude.

• Get in the game where you can lose, fail, get mussed up, pushed around, judged, evaluated, compared, and be told no. It's actually more fun than listening to your ego and playing it safe and small in the stands.

• Battle the illusion of fear created by the ego. Be calm in the face of negative thoughts and feelings, and resolutely find a more empowering perspective.

- Make your calls early in the day. You will feel the positive energy from your efforts the rest of the day.

- SWx3 = "Some will, some won't, so what." Zig Ziglar.

- Don't let your creativity keep you from doing your required activities.

- Who do you call first? Dial with reckless abandon or pick and choose—it doesn't matter. Just dial someone and then dial another.

- Be solution-oriented, not doubt-oriented.

- You must believe you have a legitimate worthwhile offer for the right person.

- Prospecting is the price you pay for your freedom.

- Prospecting is the price you pay for your income.

- Lack of interest is not a negative reflection on you or your product.

- Fun is no expectations while winning some of the time.

- What makes things more fun? When you can't lose no matter what happens. When you dial the phone with the right attitude, you can't lose.

- The people who are the most successful fail the most.

- Find a reason to call people, not a reason not to.

- Find a reason to call them now!

- You have to roll the dice to be in the game.

- It doesn't matter what happens on any one call.

- You get paid to dial, not by people's response.

- It's simple: you make calls, you make money.

- As a Relationship Builder, you are calling to see who you connect with more than who you can sell.

- The guts to dial the phone and make an offer is required.

- Prospecting is a contact sport.

- The most fun way to approach phoning is to make it an improv performance.

- The most successful prospectors live on the phone.

- On the phone, attitude is everything.

- This is easy work without the ego's negative baggage.

- This is easy work once you get past the fear of being judged.

- You don't know who people are until you call! Even if your ego thinks it knows, it doesn't.

- When you prospect, you get paid well to let a few people judge you.

- The important part of "Just Do It" which is implied, is to stop thinking and just do it!

- Create a positive anticipation; the next call could be your next client.

- As a Relationship Builder, your clients will be obvious.

- Choose to do the required activities rather than avoid them.

- You are calling to see if you can help in some way.

- What creates the resistance? The moment of being judged. If you eliminate the fear of the judgment, you have no fear of phoning.

- Have more fun fishing for ideal clients.

- If you are afraid of running out of people to call, your ego has taken over.

- When you dial the phone, you win no matter what happens.

- If you suspend all negative judgments, you freeze the power of your scared, controlling ego to keep you off the phone.

- If you prospect with skill, you control your income and your freedom. Is that worth a little discomfort?

- The act of dialing the phone can be extremely powerful. It's been said that the flutter of butterfly wings can start a hurricane.

- This is relatively easy work for good money. Be thankful for this job.

- The act of dialing the phone and making an offer is actually a tiny effort.

- You get paid more to spend more time failing.

- The only way to fail at prospecting is not to do it.

- "The chest you are most afraid to open holds the greatest treasure." *(Anonymous.)*

– *SPIRIT-BASED* –

- The cure for your doubt is to have faith and trust in all the calls you make, not just the good ones.

- Suspend your ego's desire to protect you from what it perceives to be a threat and realize that there is nothing to fear if you are connected to your Higher Self.

- When you are connected to your Higher Self, you will discover confidence and competence.

- Golf analogy: if you are not trusting your intuitive instincts to hit the shot, you are not going to hit well.

- You only really control your actions and your attitude; the rest is up to God.

- Fear or resistance means the ego is involved. The ego lives in the past and the future. Turn down the volume of the ego voice by getting into the present moment and focusing on the quiet, intuitive spirit. Your intuitive spirit lives only in the now and has no fear.

- Be a demonstration of a loving, intuitive spirit instead of a scared, controlling ego, both in prospecting and in living your life.

- Prospecting creates mystical momentum. It's like the Universe is watching to see if you make your calls. If you make the effort with the right attitude, the Universe will send some business your way.

- Let God handle the details. All you have to do is dial the phone and trust that what you are guided to do is connected to God's Presence. It helps to have an idea of what you are going to say, but the more you can trust, the more you can wing it.

- If you do what you are guided to do, you will be helped.

- Follow the subtle, quiet voice of your intuitive spirit, not your controlling ego.

- God can make anything work in ways you never imagined.

- I suspend my ego's desire to control, push, or lead people to a predetermined conclusion. My job as an intuitive spirit is to help people make an informed decision that feels right to them. If you take this approach, you will be helped in unexpected ways.

- Does it feel intuitively right to make prospecting calls? Does it feel right to be representing this product? If the answers are yes, you will be helped. Some will call it luck; you will come to know different.

- God decides who your clients are. It's called God's Selection Process.

- Say no to doubt and negative judgment and yes to trust and faith in God's Selection Process.

- Be fearless: trust the luck of the draw guided by the unseen power of God's Selection Process.

- What matters is that you make enough calls for God's Selection Process to work in your favor.

- Trust whatever happens. How people respond is exactly how they are supposed to respond. If you are being a good person making a decent offer and they respond negatively, they have deselected themselves with God's Selection Process. Don't give it another thought. Make the next call.

- Don't judge God's Selection Process.

- If you negatively judge God's Selection Process, you are not trusting God. Do you think you can do this better than God? Your ego does!

- No negative thoughts or feelings, only trust and faith in God's Selection Process.

- If you don't make calls, you are not giving God ways to give you what you want.

- Give God something to work with by creating new relationships from prospecting.

- Dear God, give me the courage to call people so I can find my clients.

- *"As ye sow, so shall ye reap."* (Corinthians)

- *"Ask, and it shall be given; seek, and ye shall find; knock, and the door shall be opened unto you."* (Luke)

EPILOGUE

It's time to jump off the cliff and discover that you knew how to fly all along. *All you have to do to win is to jump into action*. It's time to do the thing you need to do. It's time to prospect!

• Create a warm-up of your favorite phrases and one-liners that shift you into the bigger perspective. Read it every day or before you make prospecting calls.

• Create your *Resource State* in the present moment and stay there for as long as possible. That's where the magic happens. Worrying about what happened in the past or what could happen in the future is a considerable distraction to the single-minded focus you need now.

• Make sure the action you are about to take feels intuitively right (it doesn't have to feel good; it just needs to feel right). Then prepare to act and stop all other thinking. Lower the *Cone of Protection* over your being and block out all negative thoughts.

• Commit to taking action no matter what you are thinking or feeling. Get all your butterflies pointed in the same direction and dive in. You can do it!

• As you dial the phone (take action), don't judge anything negatively. If you find you're having negative thoughts and feelings, ask yourself for their positive counterparts and write them down while the phone is ringing. I do this all the time—it works. It's like *fencing with your ego*. The good news is that *you* are the chooser, not your ego. Your ability to cut off your ego's power source is only a thought away.

• *You will forget all this great advice and feel like you're stuck again.* That's normal. Your ego doesn't want you to remember that you are in charge and can be unstoppable in the face of resistance. Your ego doesn't want you to remember your breakthroughs or the power you have to override its advice. Your ego wants to hold back, coast, avoid discomfort, avoid failure, avoid looking bad, avoid being wrong, and live a life of privilege and luxury without expending any effort. Your ego does not want to mess with menial things like doing your work.

• You have to choose to believe in your Self, because your ego is always going to be worried, skeptical, and doubtful of your ability (this can also manifest as overconfidence). Your ego will never have the capacity to see who you really are, nor can it see the massive resources behind you when you take action as an intuitive spirit.

• There is a simple shortcut to this whole process that is always there. *The shortcut is to act*, to dive in, to dial the phone, to make your offer, to pop the question, to say what you need to say, or to do whatever it is you need to do.

• *This reality favors the doer of what feels intuitively right toward a positive vision.* Fortunes have been created with this simple focus. Do the thing you need to do—prospect—and you will find your pieces of gold!

• *Being able to do what you need to do, to get what you want, is the single most important skill you can develop.* You can have a lot of dents in your armor, but if you can't fight off your ego and find the courage to take action, you're toast. The quality of your life depends on your ability to act.

In the words of Abraham Lincoln, "Always bear in mind that your own resolution to succeed is more important than any other one thing."

APPENDIX

THE QUALITIES OF EGO VS. SPIRIT

EGO:	SPIRIT:
• False self created by other people's opinions of you.	• Real self accessed from your intuition, conscience, and soul.
• Has an illusion of separation from Source.	• One with the Source/God/Universe.
• Created from birth forward by what you perceive others think of you.	• You are born with your Spirit Self intact. It is complete and ready for a new life.
• Focused on survival and the assurance of survival.	• Focused on fulfilling its visions, purpose, mission, calling.
• Has a fear you might not survive.	• Doesn't think negative thoughts.
• Lives in the past and the future.	• Lives in the present moment.
• Data is based on past experience.	• Data source immeasurable, total recall.
• Likes status quo/comfort zone, resistant to change, innovation, and creativity.	• Confident in ability to adapt and find workable solutions to any challenge.
• Looks for what is wrong and what could go wrong.	• Assumes you will be shown how to succeed in any situation.
• Constantly judging and evaluating.	• Listens for what feels intuitively right.

EGO:	SPIRIT:
• External focus for information.	• Internal focus for information.
• Controlling; needs to be right about the information it has collected or believes.	• Flowing; looks for what feels intuitively right, or what works with good for all.
• Tries to protect you from what is happening or could happen.	• Focused on responding appropriately in the present moment.
• Tries to avoid mistakes.	• Sees mistakes as required to succeed.
• Sees a scarcity of resources.	• Sees an abundance of resources.
• Gets analytical under pressure, wants observable proof before taking action.	• Trusts life's process. Trusts that an answer or solution will appear in time.
• Trusts observable proof and the five physical senses.	• Intuition trumps intellect for direction and timing. Recognizes unseen influences.
• Exclusive: "You OR me."	• Inclusive: "You AND me."
• Limited creativity within a framework.	• Unlimited imagination and creativity.
• Scared, cautious.	• Fearless, undaunted.
• Fun is coasting, being entertained.	• Fun is challenge, innocent pleasures.

CREATIVE QUESTIONS TO PONDER

A lot of things in life appear to be totally out of our control. However, we seem to have a say about *some* of the things that happen in our lives because of our creative ability. Quantum scientists keep uncovering new versions of this theme. *Some say our creative ability is far more powerful than we ever imagined.*

Two fascinating concepts from Quantum Physics stand out. One, solid matter is not really solid but mostly space and energy. Could that be a form of intention? Two, at the smallest possible level that we can see, what we see changes depending on who is looking at it. *In other words, what you think you see is what gets created!* I wonder how much of that we are doing?

However it works, a great way to jump-start the creative process is to ask yourself a question. Then you can see what pops into your mind or go deeper and ask yourself, "What do I *really* want to create?" "What feels intuitively right to me?"

Here is a list of questions to get you started. The real list is endless.

What do I want to see?

What do I want to feel?

What do I want to experience?

What do I want to experience once?

What do I want to experience more than once?

What do I want to experience on a regular basis?

What do I want to touch?

What do I want to taste?

What do I want to smell?

What do I want to witness?

What do I want to do?

What do I want to master?

What do I want to be good at?

What do I want to learn?

What do I want to study?

What do I want to maintain?

What do I want to grow?

What do I want to stop doing?

What do I want to enhance in my life?

What do I want more of?

What do I want less of?

What do I want to get rid of?

What do I want to give up?

What do I want to add to my life?

What do I want that I don't have?

What would make me happy?

What would empower me?

What would be an outrageous goal for me that somehow feels right?

What do I really want to feel, and what do I need to do to feel that?

Write down the answers and any other questions that popped into your head as you read this list. Those are usually important clues.

FAVORITE RESOURCES

Books by Paramahansa Yogananda (Yogananda-SRF.org): My favorite spiritual author and meditation resource, brilliantly clear and understandable. Many practical books, booklets, and audio on how to live life to its fullest. Self-Realization Fellowship is the organization in the US.

Landmark Education (LandmarkEducation.com): Group training on how to be more effective in fulfilling what's important to you by having more power, freedom, and full self-expression. They don't advertise—you have to be invited. There is a free presentation by a master trainer every month in major cities. You are now officially invited to check out this resource. Seriously consider doing the initial training, called *The Forum.* It is a weekend everyone should experience. The basic training is now being taught in nine languages in over thirty countries. The Landmark Curriculum is one of the most powerful training programs for learning to do what you need to do.

Motivation Management Service (theMMS.com): *New York Times* best-selling author Dr. Cherie Carter Scott and her sister Lynn Stewart are my intuitive coaching mentors. They have been leaders in the coaching field since 1975 and are experts on how to get past negativity, blocked feelings, and the barriers to finding your authentic self.

Books by Steven Pressfield: *The War of Art—Break Through the Blocks and Win Your Inner Creative Battles; Do The Work; Turning Pro;* and *The Legend of Bagger Vance*, subsequently produced as a feature film by Robert Redford starring Will Smith, Matt Damon, and Charlize Theron.

Books by Timothy Gallwey: *The Inner Game of Tennis, The Inner Game of Golf,* and *Inner Skiing.* Sports coach and business consultant with a profound and practical understanding of the power of intuition.

Books by Eric Butterworth: *In the Flow of Life* and *Spiritual Economics*. A revered author in my library. Eric was a Unity minister in Detroit who had thousands attending his service every Sunday. A master of "staying in the flow," backing it all up with scripture.

You Can't Afford the Luxury of a Negative Thought — A Book for People with Any Life-Threatening Illness Including Life by Peter McWilliams. A comprehensive encyclopedia on positive thinking endorsed by both Oprah Winfrey and Larry King.

ABOUT THE AUTHOR

SIDNEY C. WALKER

Sid Walker is a pioneer, an innovator, and a seeker of empowering solutions to the challenges we face in sales and communication.

As an executive outplacement coach, Sid had several Fortune 500 clients by age twenty-eight. Hearing a call to expand his coaching skills, Sid found *New York Times* best-selling author Dr. Cherie Carter Scott, who is considered the mother of coaching. Sid was certified as a coach by her training company, Motivation Management Service (theMMS.com), in 1982.

In 1988, Sid wrote his first book, *Trusting YourSelf* (updated to *Trust Your Gut* in 2004). He then focused on the financial services industry as a coach. Sid has coached more than 2,000 advisors. He is the founder of SellingWithoutWrestling.com, an extensive training site for advisors who are advocates of the low-key or no sales pressure approach. A large percentage of Sid's coaching clients have become sales production leaders in their respective fields.

Sid has written a collection of nonfiction softcover books, ebooks, and hundreds of articles. His best-selling book is *How to Double Your Sales by Asking a Few More Questions.*

After rising to the leadership level of many contemporary training programs and thousands of hours as a sales performance coach to many talented and gifted people, Sid found the message he wants to share. Teach entrepreneurs, business owners, and salespeople how to move away from the restrictions of the selfish, limited ego and develop a stronger relationship with their boundless, intuitive spirit. The plan is to continue to coach, speak, and write books on this topic.

Sid currently has an individual coaching practice and does periodic tele-webinars and limited speaking engagements. For current contact info, go to:

www.SidWalker.com

OPT-IN TO MAILING LIST

If you would like invitations to *free webinars*, *periodic articles*, and *new product announcements*, opt-in to our mailing list at:

www.ConquerCallReluctance.com

Privacy Policy: We will not give out your email or contact information for any reason. You can cancel your subscription at anytime.

OTHER BOOKS BY SIDNEY C. WALKER

– Nonfiction –

TRUST YOUR GUT — *How to Overcome the Obstacles to Greater Success and Self-fulfillment*

HOW TO DOUBLE YOUR SALES BY ASKING A FEW MORE QUESTIONS — *Making More Sales by Helping People Get What THEY Really Want*

THE PROSPECTING MENTALITY — *How to Overcome Call Reluctance, Procrastination, and Sleepless Nights*

HOW TO GET MORE COMFORTABLE ASKING FOR REFERRALS

– Visionary Fiction –

THE LIGHTSPACE ULTIMATUM — EVOLVE OR DIE

HIRE SID AS YOUR COACH

Dear Reader,

I like to tell people you don't need to hire a coach. You will eventually figure out how to succeed as long as you don't quit. The reason you hire a coach is to speed up the process. I can cut years off the learning curve and have saved a lot of careers by helping people increase their sales within a few weeks.

My specialty is financial advisors primarily because they have one of the most challenging sales jobs. When you are selling intangible products like investments and life insurance, the product doesn't sell itself because it's usually just a piece of paper. You have to trust the advisor. I am an expert on how to create a meaningful level of trust in the first interview.

My clients include financial advisors, coaches, consultants, product reps, MLM, entrepreneurs, business owners, inventors, professionals, career changers, and retiring professional athletes.

I'm a champion of the low-key approach, which is to help your client figure out what they want and then help them get it without sales pressure. I have created a lot of millionaires who lead their companies in sales and don't use any sales techniques whatsoever!

If you want to explore the possibility of working together, send me an email with your contact info so we can set up a time to talk. We can get to know each other a little and see if we might be a good match for a coaching project.

Kind regards,

Sid@SidWalker.com

WRITE A REVIEW

It's easy and it's good karma!

With thousands of books being published every day, getting a positive review is a bigger deal to authors than you might think. In the online world, the success of a book is greatly influenced by the number of positive reviews.

If you like something about a book, write a review. A couple of sentences are all you need, along with a subject line. Of course, you can write more.

Answer any of the following questions and you've got a review...

• What did you like about the book?

• What did you find valuable about the book?

• What positive experience did you get from reading the book?

• What did you relate to the most?

• What moved you?

• What made you feel something important?

• What insight(s) did you get from reading the book?

• Did the book change how you will approach life in any way?

• Was there anything different about this book that you liked?

• Does this book remind you of any other book(s) you have read?

The authors of the world collectively thank you for your thoughtfulness and generosity!